Placing Students at the Heart of Creative Learning

Placing Students at the Heart of Creative Learning shows teachers of Key Stages 2 and 3 how to introduce creativity into what is often seen as a prescriptive and stifling curriculum, and addresses the tensions that can exist between the requirement to follow the curriculum and the desire to employ innovative pedagogies. It offers readers a range of practical and realistic ways that curriculum-changing ideas can be applied to individual projects, classrooms and even entire schools.

This book tracks the imaginative initiatives undertaken by six schools as they have worked to change their curriculum and teaching in order to put student experiences at the core of the learning process. Stating its observations and suggestions in a refreshingly straightforward and practicable manner, this book explores:

- why a new creative curriculum is needed for the twenty-first century;
- how to encourage teachers and pupils to 'own' the curriculum;
- the role that pupil voice plays in a creative curriculum;
- the environment needed to creatively manipulate the curriculum;
- how to introduce innovation to teaching practice;
- what actually works – considering the limits and possibilities of creative pedagogy.

Providing case studies and examples of the ways in which teachers have delivered the curriculum in a creative way, *Placing Students at the Heart of Creative Learning* is an invaluably beneficial guide for all those involved in engaging and teaching young people in Key Stages 2 and 3.

Nick Owen is Director of the Aspire Trust, an Arts and Creative Industries Development Agency based in Liverpool and the Wirral, UK.

Creative Teaching/Creative Schools Series

Series Editors: Pat Thomson, Julian Sefton-Green and Naranee Ruthra-Rajan

Placing Students at the Heart of Creative Learning

Edited by Nick Owen

Routledge
Taylor & Francis Group

LONDON AND NEW YORK

First published 2012
by Routledge
2 Park Square, Milton Park, Abingdon, Oxon OX14 4RN

Simultaneously published in the USA and Canada
by Routledge
711 Third Avenue, New York, NY 10017

Routledge is an imprint of the Taylor & Francis Group, an informa business

British Library Cataloguing in Publication Data
A catalogue record for this book is available from the British Library

Library of Congress Cataloging in Publication Data
Owen, Nick.
    Placing students at the heart of creative learning / Nick Owen.
        p. cm.
    1. Creative teaching. 2. Creative ability. 3. Classroom environment. I. Title.
    LB1044.88.O94 2012
    371.102′4—dc22   2011016292

ISBN: 978–0–415–56999–6 (hbk)
ISBN: 978–0–415–57001–5 (pbk)
ISBN: 978–0–203–81808–4 (ebk)

Typeset in Galliard
by Swales & Willis Ltd, Exeter, Devon

Printed and bound in Great Britain by
TJ International Ltd, Padstow, Cornwall

Contents

Illustrations

Series Introduction

We live in creative times. As political aspiration, as economic driver, as a manifesto for school reform and curriculum change, the desire for creativity can be found across the developed world in policy pronouncements and academic research. But creativity in schools can mean many things: turning classrooms into more exciting experiences, curriculum into more thoughtful challenges, teachers into different kinds of instructors, assessment into more authentic processes and putting young people's voice at the heart of learning. In general, these aspirations are motivated by two key concerns – to make experience at school more exciting, relevant, challenging and dynamic; and ensuring that young people are able to contribute to the creative economy which will underpin growth in the twenty-first century.

Transforming these common aspirations into informed practice is not easy. Yet there are programmes, projects and initiatives which have consistently attempted to offer change and transformation. There are significant creativity programmes in many parts of the world, including France, Norway, Canada, South Korea, Australia and the United States of America. The English programme, Creative Partnerships (www.creative-partnerships.com) is the largest of these and this series of books draws on its experience and expertise.

This book, *Placing Students at the Heart of Creative Learning*, is published as part of a series of books, 'Creative Teaching/Creative Schools'. The series is written for head teachers, curriculum co-ordinators and classroom practitioners who are interested in creative learning and teaching. Each book offers principles for changing classroom and school practice and stimulus material for CPD sessions. The emphasis is on practical, accessible studies from real schools, framed by jargon-free understandings of key issues and the principles found in more academic studies. Each volume contains six detailed 'case studies' written by practising teachers and other creative practitioners, each describing a project they have introduced in their schools. These stories are complemented by accounts from learners themselves, making clear the benefit and value of these approaches to changing learning.

What is creative learning?

When educators talk about creative learning they generally mean teaching which allows students to use their imaginations, have ideas, generate multiple possible solutions to problems, communicate in a variety of media and in general 'think outside the box'. They may also mean practices in which children and young people show that they have the capacities to assess and improve work, sustain effort on a project for a long period of time, exceed what they thought was possible and work well with others to combine ideas and approaches. Some may extend the notion to include projects and approaches which allow young people to apply their creativity through making choices about what and how they will learn, negotiating about curriculum and involvement in generating possibilities for and making decisions about school priorities and directions.

But while there may be commonalities about what creative learning looks like as and in students' behaviours, there may also be profound differences. The notion of creativity may be associated with particular subjects, such as those that go under the umbrella term of the arts, in which generating new, odd and interesting perspectives on familiar topics is valued and rewarded. Or it may be seen as integral to science, where habits of transforming curiosity into hypotheses have a long history. Or it may be connected to business and the goal of schooling students to have strongly entrepreneurial dispositions and capacities. These interpretations – and many more – are all possible and legitimate understandings of creativity and creative learning.

Although the term 'creative learning' may be new and fashionable, it draws on older knowledge and values which have helped give it legitimacy and which frame its current meaning; see *The Routledge International Handbook of Creative Learning* (Sefton-Green *et al.*, 2011) and *Researching Creative Learning: Methods and Issues* (Thomson and Sefton-Green, 2010).

We have expressed our understanding of creative learning as a series of 'manifesto' principles. They underpin all the volumes in this series. Students' creative learning depends on a quality of education where:

- All young people from every kind of background are equally recognised as being creative.
- Learning engages young people in serious, meaningful, relevant, imaginative and challenging activities and tasks.
- Young people are respected for their knowledge, experience and capabilities.
- Young people have an individual and collective right to actively shape their education.
- Teachers have the power to support, adapt and evaluate learning experiences for students exercising their professional judgement.
- Schools invest in teacher learning.
- Schools build partnerships with creative individuals and organisations.
- Schools enable young people to participate fully in social and cultural worlds.
- Families and local communities can play an inspiring and purposeful role in young people's learning.

Pat Thomson, Julian Sefton-Green and Naranee Ruthra-Rajan

Contributors

Alison Burrowes, Thornleigh Salesian College, Bolton
Alistair Chambers, Kingstone School, Barnsley
Sarah Coxon, Dale Primary School, Derby
Iain Erskine, Fulbridge Primary School, Peterborough
Mandie Heywood, Old Park Primary School, Telford
Mick Johnson, Thornleigh Salesian College, Bolton
Charlotte Krzanicki, Fulbridge Primary School, Peterborough
Nick Owen, Aspire Trust, Liverpool
Chris Reck, Belfairs High School, Southend
Julian Sefton-Green, Special Professor of Education, University of Nottingham
Pat Thomson, Professor of Education, University of Nottingham

Acknowledgements

The editor would like to express his admiration for the inspiring work of the school leaders who contributed to this book, and to thank them for their assistance and support. It was a privilege to visit the schools that provided the case studies.

Gratitude is also extended to the series editors and editorial team for their guidance and encouragement.

Introduction

Julian Sefton-Green, Pat Thomson and Nick Owen

This book describes the imaginative initiatives undertaken by six schools as they have worked to change their curriculum and teaching in order to put student experiences at the heart of learning. It offers readers an account of the practical ways in which projects, classrooms and indeed whole schools accommodate and develop ideas to change curriculum. But the book also canvasses some important reasons for putting student experiences at the heart of learning, as well as making a hard-headed appraisal of 'what works' – and what doesn't – considering the limits and possibilities of such approaches.

This introduction sets out some of the key ideas and themes that you will encounter through the case study chapters that follow. The cases have been compiled by the editor of this volume, together with key teachers and creative practitioners, to describe extensive, ambitious and complex change initiatives across a range of schools. Each chapter explains a different approach to developing creative learning and offers a series of reflective questions and professional development activities to explore these ideas in greater detail and to make them applicable for your school. A final section at the end of the book offers a series of professional development experiences suitable for whole school or department work.

Here we outline the main themes of the book and then describe how each chapter exemplifies these key themes. We conclude by briefly explaining how the book was put together by a number of contributors and offer suggestions for ways in which different readers can use the book as they seek to apply its lessons to their own circumstances or further work.

The work described in this book was mainly developed as part of the English programme Creative Partnerships.

From student experiences to curriculum reform

All of the case studies collected in this book argue that both what and how students learn needs in some ways to stem from, and engage with, their life experiences. This ambition covers a range of theoretical and practical challenges.

In recent years the idea of 'personalisation' has received much attention and even became the object of policy development through the now defunct Qualifications and Curriculum Authority. This is but one contemporary element in a complex policy picture and we discuss it in some detail later in this introduction. At the same time as the term personalisation gained popularity, attacks on simple and naïve versions of 'experiential' learning – allegedly popular in forms of now discredited 1960s progressivism – regularly appear in the newspapers and in the mouths of politicians condemning trendy teaching (Jones, 2003). In these attacks and critiques teachers allegedly substitute student experience for the discipline of formal academic knowledge. We will see below how this simplistic binary opposition between accepted curriculum knowledge and student experience is neither a helpful way to think about teaching/learning, nor a formulation that any of the schools and teachers represented in this book actually use.

The relationships between experience, learning, knowledge and pedagogy are complex and deep. They are rooted in often implicit conceptualisations of how people learn, how knowledge itself is created, maintained and transmitted and how we construct curriculum and how we believe teaching works. According to Kieran Egan, despite the plethora of overwhelming initiatives, there are in fact only two or three really big ideas in education about how people learn that have endured (Egan, 1997), and we highlight some of these in the next subsection: Learning and experience. Much of what we know about the principles that underpin teaching and learning is derived from the work of John Dewey and Lev Vygotsky undertaken in the early part of the twentieth century, and so we devote some time to them here.

Of course, whilst it is possible just to think about experience in terms of what it means to each of us as individuals, collective experience also produces its own kind of knowledge. In their studies of schooling of Hispanic minorities in the US Southwest, Luis Moll and his colleagues developed the concept of 'funds of knowledge' to explain how experiences derived out of school can be progressively developed in concert with an open-minded school curriculum, and that the more school and out-of-school 'know' about each other, the more purposeful and effective curriculum is (Gonzalez *et al.*, 2005). This is examined in depth below. Funds of knowledge approaches are of course profoundly social and community focused in their outlook and there is a long tradition of examining how education needs to be preparing young people for participation in forms of community and civic life and this is our third key theme.

Many teachers know that, irrespective of the politics of experience and its relationship with formal curriculum knowledge, there is a range of different practical ways in which such ideas influence how young people engage in learning. This link between students' engagement and experience is more explicitly developed in a sister publication to this book, *Turning Pupils onto Learning: Creative Classrooms in Action*, by Rob Elkington. Here we touch on dimensions related to developing the learning self, that is, how developing curriculum from experience can support learners to become more confident, trusting and prepared to engage in study. Finally, we critically review the 'ideology' of personalisation, both exploring what it offers to current activities in the classroom and also casting a critical eye on some of the limiting ways it frames the challenge of individual experience.

Learning and experience

Philosophers have long been vexed by the challenges of understanding how human beings, who fundamentally utilise sensory experience to make sense of the world, can create 'objective' forms of knowledge through language in ways that appear to transcend our senses and our immediate experience. Contemporary thinkers largely agree that the quest for 'objectivity' is fruitless and that there is no escaping the reality that, as a species, we inevitably make meaning of the world through cultural practices, and ultimately through our particular and situated experiences. Scholars of human development have to engage with these larger philosophical questions as they seek to explain how the growing child can build an understanding of the world though their immediate (that is, direct and sensory) and/or mediated (that is, verbal, number, movement or visual language) experiences (Rogoff, 2003). Indeed, all notions of schooling are built on some kind of supposition about how this meaning-making process actually works and how different children of different ages might or might not need access to varying types of mediating experiences in order to make sense of their lives and the wider world.

The Russian psychologist Lev Vygotsky, best known for his formulation of scaffolding and the zone of proximal development (ZPD), offers a coherent and widely accepted theory of how we use experience recursively as a way of making sense of the world, in concert with direct instruction and the use of language (Vygotsky, 1978; Vygotsky, 2002):

■ Scaffolding refers to the construction of supported 'steps' that allow the learner to attain knowledge/skills. This might take the form of direct or indirect instruction, sequencing and pacing of activities, or the provision of affordances – particular materials, activities and events – in the learning environment. There are significant debates about the degree of scaffolding that children need, with some suggesting that all or particular children need tight scripting, while others opt for a much more open-ended approach. Most teachers offer a mix of tight and open scaffolding. Creative learning approaches provide a wider repertoire of these more exploratory approaches, often placing particular emphasis on the affordances of the learning environment, that is, on a wide range of experiences from which meanings can be made.

■ ZPD refers to the difference between what a learner can do without help and what they can do with guidance. The teacher's task is to organise learning so that the student is situated in the ZPD, not outside it. Thus, teachers need to know what their students can do. This means more than what they have been taught in the formal curriculum, and also what they know from their everyday lives, being who they are and where they are. However, ZPDs also allow students to help each other through observing and copying and through joint activities which are either planned or occur naturally. The teaching strategies of peer and cross-age tutoring and various forms of group work all rely on students' pooling of expertise and experience through new, shared experiences in a ZPD.

Some aspects of these theories are pertinent for the chapters which follow. First of all, Vygotsky suggested that as we begin to understand the world we make sense of it by developing what he called 'spontaneous concepts'. These are theories, or perhaps pre-theories, which explain aspects of the social and physical world. Through instruction, iterative testing of these spontaneous concepts and, above all, through the application of an objective language, these spontaneous concepts get transformed into 'scientific concepts' and Vygotsky meant these to describe the social as much as the physical world. It is scientific concepts which form the basis of curriculum knowledge in that they are common, shared and can de described in objective ways that we can all make sense of – as opposed to the initially individual way the growing child makes sense of his or her world.

Vygotsky makes a clear case that there are times when we all need input from the outside – that we can't learn everything simply by ourselves or through experience – and is insistent about the role of teachers and direct instruction. He was especially interested in how language, as something that is produced outside of the individual and is socially produced, allows the growing mind to use forms of external mediation to categorise, conceptualise, model, describe and interpret sensory phenomena. This, then, is a complex picture of human social development and clearly shows that experience is not a simple category, but depends on how we make sense of it, what language we have for understanding it and whether we can relate one experience to other experiences and understandings so that we can turn experience into thought and learning. However, Vygotsky realised that turning spontaneous concepts into scientific concepts can occur only when conditions are right, and to an extent this varies between individuals. The ZPD describes a situation where individuals are, as it were, ready to learn and where instruction and other kinds of interventions can turn spontaneous concepts into scientific concepts.

Student experiences, then, are not simply a question of privileging subjective views of the world or developing a curriculum that revolves around the child or young person's view of the world. They are about children acquiring culturally accepted definitions and ways of understanding, working from what they already know to what they do not.

However, most kinds of schooling around the world pay lip-service to this notion of learning, and in fact offer forms of knowledge and pedagogies that generally do not take into account the kinds of social interactional and reflective process Vygotsky outlines.

John Dewey, the American education reformer, was highly critical of the methods adopted by mass schooling, on two key grounds. First, he argued that the activities of learning themselves needed to be more experiential in the sense of involving more sensory input and more variety in activities than simply the transmission of abstract symbolic information. His second argument was that the purposes of education should be more oriented to the lifeworlds of children and young people – both in the sense of drawing on the experiences of young people, and also of enabling young people to act in democratic society in general. More specifically, he argued for an education that would support young people to act in their workplaces and their immediate local communities.

Dewey suggested that educators generally thought about curriculum as being oppo-sitional to students' life experiences. They thus mistakenly interpreted ideas about experiential learning to mean abandoning the formal curriculum. Dewey proposed that instead of thinking of curriculum as being the opposite of students' experiences it should be thought of as a continuum. Teachers could start at any point – with what students already know from the formal curriculum or from their everyday lives or from some mix of the two – but they must, in order for the students to understand what they were doing, connect the two. The process of connection, Dewey argued, ought also to be thought of as an experience which needs to be further articulated in order to make sense to the student. Simply connecting the formal curriculum and the students' lifeworld is insufficient. Simply doing something in order to make that link is insufficient. The connection and the doing need to be formalised through language into some more accessible and replicable form – through language, action or the use of another symbolic system such as number of images. He then made this layering of learning as experience even more complex by arguing that the purpose of all of this experience is not learning for its own sake, but needs in some way to be connected to the project of living well in the world.

Funds of knowledge

One of the observations Dewey made about how schools work in practice was, as we have suggested, that there was/is a severe disjuncture between what children learn at home and out of school and what is on offer in the classroom. School tends to proscribe or ignore a huge range of life experiences and, in many cases, highly 'learned' skills. This gap or break between what children know, learn and can do as a result of their life experiences and what schools ask of them is not, then, a new tension in education. Nevertheless, it is a tension that schools have to cope with every day. The challenge is different in relation to older young people, where often it is cultural experiences that get counterposed with school learning (Sefton-Green, 2006). However, learning at home is often a key issue in early years and primary education. It is interesting to consider why and how understanding and sympathy for this principle tends to dissipate as young people grow older.

The question of what children learn out of school has also been galvanised by challenges to mainstream norms and expectations from the presence of immigrant minority communities across the Western world. Not only does the presence of bilingual children in many inner-city schools offer an extraordinary richness of language, knowledge and skills to the mainstream, it also brings into contrast the host of other kinds of educational practices that go in the home. As noted at the beginning of this introduction, working with the largely Mexican Latino/a communities in the US Southwest, Luis Moll and his colleagues developed a series of activities to bring these communities into the schools and to enable staff and parents to learn more from each other. This attention to issues of home language use, bilingualism and the range of cultural and social practices learned by children and 'taught' within the pedagogies of the home led to the articulation of the idea of a 'fund of knowledge' (Gonzalez *et al.*, 2005).

The principle here is to turn unstated, implicit and tacit practice and knowledge into 'knowledge' in the same way that the school curriculum builds on accepted knowledge about the past to devise, say, a history or science curriculum. What Moll and his colleagues did was not only to find ways to enable minority communities give their lifeworld practices the status of knowledge, but also to work with schools and parents groups to turn that home-knowledge into curriculum, so that teachers and schools had to learn what their students knew as if it was unknown knowledge – just as curriculum might appear to students.

Teachers working in indigenous communities do more than use local knowledges as a bridge to the formal curriculum; they also work to change what counts as the curriculum itself. In Australia, for example, the notion of 'two way' education recognises that very powerful learning occurs when activities are structured so that teachers learn traditional knowledges and skills at the same time as students are learning European knowledges and skills.

Although funds of knowledge is a generative concept and has several applications in education, there is obviously a long tradition in England of working with young children's home experiences as a way of building on what is brought to the school and supporting learning across what has become a more porous boundary than in Dewey's time. Notions of local and family literacies, for example, used in both the early years and adult literacy programmes, rely on teachers rejecting the notion that students come to school with deficit repertoires – no books at home, unable to read a form. Instead, they explore what literate practices exist in homes and communities – reading signs, catalogues, television advertisements, computer games and so on – and use those as the platform to connect formal literacy with what students already know and can do (Barton and Hamilton, 1998).

The learning self

One of the key intangibles that many teachers will recognise from experience, but that is much more difficult to prove through research or theory, is how curriculum and pedagogy which place the student experience more centrally, at the heart of the process, often support diverse students and different ways of learning. Not all students learn in the same way and many students have capacities, needs, interests and experiences that are neglected in school. Teaching everyone as if they were all the same is a recipe for some to miss out. Teachers must find ways to adapt mandated curriculum to the specific children and young people in their care.

Using the young person as the starting-point for activity often gives them different kinds of stake in the study and manifests different kinds of social behaviours. These can include increased confidence, better trust between student and teacher and high degrees of engagement in the course of study. Two sister publications in this series develop these ideas in more detail. Rob Elkington looks at how to develop motivation and engagement in learning and Helen Manchester explores initiatives to develop student voice. All three texts take up the challenge for many schools and teachers to find ways to engage and motivate young people.

Case studies in this book show how schools have developed curriculum or ways of approaching the curriculum at a level of structural organisation. This means how teaching groups have been constructed, how learners are addressed and offered different kinds of activities, how projects have been devised and implemented and how creative activities have been integrated with other curriculum imperatives. The teachers who have written about these projects have, naturally enough, paid attention to the way in which these kinds of re-organisation have impacted on the behaviours of the learners themselves. The need to vary approaches to teaching has been recognised as one of the most significant challenges in schooling. Policy makers offer a range of solutions: grouping students in order to reduce diversity via tracking or ability grouping – setting, for example. Other approaches include various forms of responding to small groups and individuals – differentiation, personalisation and negotiation, for example. We deal with four of these below as a means of illustrating the challenges and possibilities of these more tailored approaches.

Learning styles

Most teachers have heard of the notion of VAK – visual, auditory and kinaesthetic learning 'styles'. There is a serious debate about whether this formulation has any grounding in research. However, some schools have found it a useful place to start to think about:

■ diversifying modes of instruction from a monotonous diet of worksheets and whiteboard notes;

■ ensuring that children have multiple genres through which to explore topics and provide evidence of their learning.

Problems arise when children are diagnosed as being a particular kind of learner, and then either are taught in that mode, which clearly prevents them from learning how to use multiple approaches to learning, or are given remedial instruction in the modes in which they are perceived to have deficits. Both of these options decelerate learning and are a deviation from the major challenge of providing variation in pedagogical approaches.

There are other theories of learning styles. David Kolb's model of learning from experience through a cycle of concrete experience, abstract conceptualisation, reflective observation and active experimentation, for example, is widely used. His diagnostic inventory of styles of learning – converger (abstract conceptualisation and active experimentation), diverger (concrete experience and reflective observation), assimilator (abstract conceptualisation and reflective observation) and accommodator (concrete experience and reflective observation) – is critiqued as having an inadequate research base, being too narrow and rigid and, like VAK, as being easily misused and thus leading to labelling of children and, subsequently, poor teaching processes and learning outcomes.

Multiple intelligences

Howard Gardner's (1993, 1999) theory of multiple intelligences operates as a powerful critique of the dominant cultural assumption that intelligence is based in a particular kind of language-based activity and can be tested through a set of language and number exercises. He posited a series of intelligences – spatial, linguistic, logical-mathematical, bodily-kinaesthetic, musical, interpersonal, intrapersonal, naturalistic and existential. While many psychologists have queried the scientific basis for this formulation, some educators have found it a helpful audit of teaching methods and the structure of curriculum. They have asked, for example, how much time is given to musical activities as opposed to those based in linguistic activities, and have worked to find pedagogies which allow students to combine learning and the expression of that learning through multiple modes. However, the same kinds of criticisms that are levelled at learning styles also apply to multiple intelligences – if they are used as a means of categorising children and teaching to that category, the results are counter-productive and inequitable, rather than enhancing inclusivity.

Learning how to learn

A number of schools have taken the view that students need to have a better grasp of their own learning processes as well as specific instruction in a set of twenty-first-century skills such as team work, thinking, managing emotions and communication. Schools believe that if students are better able to understand their own metacognition and relationships, then they will be more self-managing independent learners. These learning to learn sets are generally offered as a stand-alone 'subject', although they can also be offered as part of a cross-curriculum activity.

Critics of this approach suggest that, contrary to common-sense interpretations, research suggests that these are largely not generic skills – thinking like a mathematician, for example, is not the same as thinking like a historian. Thus, these kinds of skills must be learned/taught in the context of specific knowledge. Guy Claxton, for example, suggests that teachers need to think about 'split screen' planning, where disciplinary knowledges sit in one column and learning to learn competencies sit in another. Activities are planned to incorporate both columns.

Personalisation

The notion of personalisation in its current form is drawn from work conducted by the think-tank Demos about the effectiveness of public services. In a pamphlet (2004), which became highly influential on the thinking of the then New Labour government, Charles Leadbeater stated that public services operated as a 'one size fits all'. This was highly ineffective, he asserted, and profoundly unsatisfying to service users. Rather than this bland uniformity, Leadbeater suggested that all public services should be bespoke tailored to the specific needs of the people who used them. The way to do this, he argued, was to get service users involved in assessing needs and designing the services, ensuring that, even though there were unique differences in approach, all services met universal quality indicators through public accountability measures.

This notion of personalisation has been championed in education by David Hargreaves through a set of work supported by the Specialist Schools and Academies Trust. Hargreaves (2004) developed the idea of 'gateways' to personalised learning – different routes that schools might take in order to make sure that 'bespoke' schooling is tailored to their particular community and student population:

- assessment for learning;
- learning to learn;
- student voice;
- curriculum characterised by deep learning, cross-curriculum activities and flexibility in timetabling;
- new technologies;
- school design and organisation with school leaders seen as organisational redesigners;
- advice and guidance;
- mentoring and coaching;
- workforce development, and in particular the use of adults other than teachers to complement the work of teachers.

Many of these 'gateways' appear in this book and they are all addressed across the series.

Regrettably, the notion of personalisation has been taken by a few schools to equate to new forms of setting and tracking. It is seen as legitimating approaches which see only some children and young people as capable of high standards, and thus justifies offering pathways with less-valued credentials and learnings to those who are deemed less 'able'. This response substitutes the fundamental notion of standards which offer valued common learning to everyone through diverse approaches for one which offers different outcomes to different students, based on their alleged capabilities. Personalisation does not mean new forms of sorting and selecting. Rather, it means precisely the reverse – new approaches to teaching/learning which offer more young people the possibilities of learning what counts and being recognised, through significant credentials, for that learning.

Creative learning is, we suggest, a key approach in the processes of inclusive and equitable personalisation. It is based in teachers' and creative practitioners' understanding of the life experiences of their students, organising learning experiences that connect those life experiences with the mandated curriculum and then articulating and generalising that connecting experience. This is accomplished using multiple media and diverse pedagogies and in conversation with students.

The purpose of this book

This book addresses the four big questions of learning styles, multiple intelligences, learning how to learn and personalisation through a series of six case studies of schools which are located in a variety of environments, from inner city to semi-rural, in Bolton, Peterborough, Telford, Barnsley, Southend and Derby. Whilst all offer insights on all four questions, each case study offers a different focus.

In Chapter 1, Fulbridge Primary School in Peterborough has developed a local, vernacular curriculum which takes as its starting-point local histories, geographies and resources as the means to galvanise children's learning. This work is based heavily upon Kolb's (1984) model of learning from experience, and demonstrates in particular how different mediums, such as sculpture, film, animation and drama can be used to explore curriculum links with writing.

In Chapter 2, Dale Primary School in Derby has looked to early years practice in the town of Pistoia, Italy as a means of providing immersive learning experiences which are engendered through its approach to 'slow pedagogy'. Its stance on personalised learning is one which allows for engagement in a curriculum which is driven by constant formative reflection, a profound knowledge of children's progression in skills and learning which is fired by children's curiosity and questions.

In Chapter 3, 'real world' learning is demonstrated by Old Park Primary School in Telford, which particularly focuses on Learning to Learn (L2L) strategies and connects its work with that of Guy Claxton's Building Learning Power programme as part of its bigger commitment to the Personalised Learning Agenda.

In Chapter 4, Belfairs High School, a secondary school in Southend, demonstrates how focusing on children as independent thinkers and learners identifies a number of strategies which encourage young people to think about, and learn from, their own learning styles. In addition to the L2L programme, the school also focuses on and embeds a particular cluster of thinking skills across the school curriculum.

In Chapter 5, Kingstone School in Barnsley adopts a thematic approach to teaching collaboratively in order to develop cross-curriculum projects which can be taught in a way that bridges the pedagogical gap that exists between the high school and its feeder primary schools. It highlights particularly the use of established drama-based teaching conventions, such as Dorothy Heathcote's Mantle of the Expert, in the humanities in order to strengthen and deepen students' understanding (Heathcote, 1984a, 1989, 2006, 2007). The chapter also shows how the personalisation agenda is reflected through project-based learning (PBL), in which teachers become able to develop alternative pedagogical strategies and teaching stances (Craft *et al.*, 2007). It builds on previous research carried out by Birmingham City University (Fautley *et al.*, 2008).

Chapter 6 demonstrates how staff at Thornleigh Salesian School, a Catholic high school in Bolton, developed programmes which were based on the concept of multiple learning styles to encourage their children's independent learning and thinking skills. The school also engaged with the Personalised Learning Agenda through programmes which focused on developing students' Learning to Learn skills, providing a new Year 7 curriculum which was characterised by deep learning, cross-curriculum activities and flexibility in timetabling, the use of new technologies and significant school redesign and organisation. It has embraced the personalised learning and thinking skills (PLTS) agenda too, but in a manner which has enabled it to take ownership of that initiative.

This book highlights some of the inspirational methods, approaches and attitudes to placing students at the heart of creative learning in a sample of primary and secondary schools across England. It shows how teachers and the wider school workforce, particularly those 'outside' the organisation, such as artists, architects and other professionals, have faced up to their local challenges, taken immense risks and fought long and hard to develop models of learning and courses of action for the children they care deeply about. In all cases in this book, these schools operate in difficult social contexts, sometimes facing parental indifference and local authority hostility, and at other times facing internal staff anxiety and negative peer pressure. But in all cases what has shone through for us, in the process of collecting the studies, reading the writings of teachers and seeing the work of young people, is what exhilarating results are produced in all these quests to innovate and transform children's learning experiences.

As well as being underpinned by the key concepts discussed at the front of this introduction, this book has been also informed by the beliefs of Dewey (1897), the criticalities of Apple (2004) and the challenge to contemporary creativity orthodoxies by writers from outside the educational milieu but whose theories offer important insights to where those orthodoxies may be taking us (Florida, 2002; Peck, 2005).

How to use this book

This book can be used to support the professional development of curriculum leaders at primary and secondary level who may be engaged in self-study, or who may be participating in more formal professional development programmes.

Reading the introduction is important because it provides the theoretical basis that underpins creative learning such as that illustrated by the case studies. Thereafter, a case study may be selected for reading, according to themes and aspects that are of particular interest. The case studies comprise a combination of teachers writing their own stories, with some adjustment, questioning and editing by the volume editor. They are presented as narratives interspersed with boxes of editorial comment and questions to aid reflection both within each chapter and at the end. Thus, the case studies may be read for interest by an individual or they may be used to prompt small-group discussion of change-leadership issues.

The final chapter of the book describes in more detail how the case studies may be used to support professional development on a group or individual basis. Four staff development sessions are provided that can be used as they are or adapted as necessary. Of course, you will also have ideas of your own about how the cases in the book might be used to stimulate the thinking of your colleagues.

However, this book is expressly not about examples of 'best practice' which can be 'disseminated' merely by reading about them. It will not provide you with a road map of 'how to get there' or 'how to do it'. One thing that shines through all the case studies here is that there is no 'bespoke' package that can be bought off a consultant's or local authority's shelf which instructs teachers on how to place children at the heart of creative learning.

This is a process which has to be bought into at first hand and committed to wholeheartedly by as many actors in the school's sphere of influence as possible, and there is no guarantee that you will come off any better as a result.

But what we hope the book does do is point out the traps, pressures, enticements and rewards. The risk is high but the rewards are great. Hopefully, the teachers who have contributed to this book will give you strategies for how to minimise the former and maximise the latter.

References

Apple, M.W. (2004) *Ideology and Curriculum*, London: Routledge.

Barton, D. and Hamilton, M. (1998) *Local Literacies: Reading and Writing in One Community*, London: Routledge.

Claxton G. (2006) *Expanding the Capacity to Learn: A New End for Education?* Warwick: British Educational Research Association Annual Conference.

Craft, A., Cremin, T., Burnard, P. and Chappell, K. (2007) 'Teacher stance in creative learning: a study of progression', *Thinking Skills and Creativity*, 2(2): 136–47.

Dewey, J. (1897) 'My pedagogic creed', *The School Journal*, 54(3): 77–80.

Egan, K. (1997) *The Educated Mind: How Cognitive Tools Shape Our Understanding*, Chicago: University of Chicago Press.

Fautley, M., Gee, M., Hatcher, R. and Millard, E. (2008) *The Creative Partnerships Curriculum Projects at Kingstone School Barnsley and Queensbridge School Birmingham*, Birmingham: Birmingham City University.

Florida, R. (2002) *The Rise of the Creative Class: And How It's Transforming Work, Leisure, Community, and Everyday Life*, New York: Basic Books.

Gardner, H. (1993) *Multiple Intelligences: The Theory in Practice*, New York: Basic Books.

Gardner, H. (1999) *Intelligence Reframed: Multiple Intelligences for the 21st Century*, New York: Basic Books.

Gonzalez, N., Moll, L.C. and Amanti, C. (2005) *Funds of Knowledge: Theorizing Practices in Households and Classrooms*, Mahwah, NJ: Lawrence Erlbaum Associates.

Hargreaves, D. (2004) *Personalised Learning: Next Steps in Working Laterally*, London: Specialist Schools Trust.

Heathcote, D. (1984) 'Signs and portents', in L. Johnson and C. O'Neill (eds) *Collected Writings*, London: Hutchinson.

Heathcote, D. (1989) 'The fight for drama: the fight for education', keynote address to the National Association for the Teaching of Drama, in K. Byron (ed.) *The Fight for Drama: The Fight for Education*, Birmingham: NATD.

Heathcote, D. (2006) Keynote address to 'A Culture for Learning', the annual conference of The National Association for the Teaching of Drama, Oxford: NATD.

Heathcote, D. (2007) 'Can stories provide contexts for working in Mantle of the Expert enterprises?', *The Journal for Drama in Education*, 23(2): 7–17.

Jones, K. (2003) *Education in Britain: 1944 to the Present*, Cambridge: Polity.

Kolb, D.A. (1984) *Experiential Learning: Experience as the Source of Learning and Development*, New Jersey: Prentice Hall.

Leadbeater, C. (2004) *Learning about Personalisation: How Can We Put the Learner at the Heart?* Available at: www.demos.co.uk or www.standards.dfes.gov.uk/innovation-unit.

Peck, J. (2005) 'Struggling with the creative class', *International Journal of Urban and Regional Research*, 29(4): 740–70.

Rogoff, B. (2003) *The Cultural Nature of Human Development*, New York: Oxford University Press.

Sefton-Green, J. (2006) 'Youth, technology and media cultures', in J. Green and A. Luke (eds) *Review of Research in Education* 30, Washington, DC: AERA, pp. 279–304.

Vygotsky, L.S. (1978) *Mind in Society: Development of Higher Psychological Processes*, Cambridge, MA: Harvard University Press.

Vygotsky, L.S. (2002) *Thought and Language*, Cambridge, MA: MIT Press.

1

The Vernacular and the Global
Fulbridge Primary School, Peterborough

Iain Erskine and Charlotte Krzanicki

Editor's introduction

The main theme of this chapter is how a school has developed a local, vernacular curriculum which takes as its starting-point local histories, geographies and resources as the means to galvanise children's learning. This work is based upon Kolb's model of learning from experience and particularly demonstrates how different mediums, such as sculpture, film, animation and drama, can be used to explore curriculum links with writing. This did not, however, lead to a situation where children were labelled as one of the four Kolb learning stylists: convergers, divergers, assimilators or accommodators. Rather, this approach enabled teachers to rethink how they could design the curriculum to meet their children's needs and interests. This curriculum – described by the schools as the Peterborough Curriculum – is characterised by:

- inspiration from local funds of knowledges and resources;
- learning from early years practice and disseminating this throughout the school;
- providing opportunities for deep-learning, cross-curriculum activities;
- flexibility in timetabling;
- ongoing redesign of school premises to support those opportunities; and
- the complementary involvement of external practitioners to support and extend the work of teachers.

The Fulbridge story demonstrates how teachers were able to adapt from a heavily prescribed way of teaching to one which was more open ended, evolutionary and, critically, reliant on the development of a creative curriculum which stemmed from what the local environment and community was able to provide. This curriculum asked a fundamental question of its teachers and pupils: 'What does Peterborough have to offer?'

Fulbridge created its own curriculum based around its locality – Peterborough – whilst simultaneously ensuring that it reflected the demands of the National Curriculum. It is in contrast to those schools that had adopted existing models of curriculum development such as Building Learning Power, Kagan Structures or drama-based frameworks such as Dorothy Heathcote's Mantle of the Expert (all models which will be referred to later in this volume).

This chapter explores two phases of curriculum reform in the school: phase one, which was generated by teachers themselves, and phase two, in which other agencies, such as CapeUK and the Creative Partnerships team, acknowledged the success of the school and contributed to its further reformative energies.

It has been written by Iain Erskine, the head teacher, from transcribed interviews. Charlotte Krzanicki, deputy head teacher, wrote the section about phase two of the development.

The backdrop to the school

The city of Peterborough provides an interesting intersection of both industrial and agricultural societies. Whilst on the one hand it has been a hub for the development of the railways after the Industrial Revolution, it is also strongly rooted in deep agricultural values with the fenlands – literally on the doorsteps of the city's residents. It consequently has for many years accommodated both long-standing, established communities and communities who have travelled from their homeland in search of work and prosperity, whether these be Italian or Pakistani communities or, more recently, communities from across Eastern Europe. At one point in the 1970s, for example, Peterborough was one of the fastest-growing cities in Europe.

This permanent flux of people in Peterborough has meant that children present teachers at Fulbridge with a particular challenge which revolves around their literacy and communication skills, knowledge of the local area and parental expectations of what school has to offer. It is not without its difficulties, either: in the local community in recent years clashes between the European and Asian communities have been reported in the local press and further afield.

A starting-point: potential organisational meltdown

Back in the early 2000s, Fulbridge Junior School was in trouble. The management of the school and children's behaviour and attainment levels were deemed unacceptable by Ofsted and the school consequently went into special measures. At the time, I was head of the attached Infant School, and when the Ofsted crunch came I was asked to take on the leadership of the Junior School. This eventually involved the closure of the two separate schools and the formation of a new school: Fulbridge Primary School. Part of my challenge involved following the necessary school inspector's guidance to take the Junior School out of special measures, but I was conscious that the heavily directive nature of this process was not necessarily the way I wanted to continue to run the new school.

I took two key decisions about developing a creative approach to our curriculum: the first, to develop a curriculum that was personalised to Fulbridge, its environment, staff and children; and the second, to design a curriculum which did not follow any particular commercial packages.

I know this was a risky strategy, but I am something of a rebel and feel that risk-taking will, more than likely, lead to success in the long run. It was important not to feel pressured to achieve short-term results but to look to the long term – to follow a four- or five-year strategy which might have been at odds with local pressures to achieve here and now.

Cast of characters/actors

Iain Erskine	Head teacher
Charlotte Krzanicki	Deputy head teacher
Roger Cole	Independent national adviser: consultant, writer and speaker
Mathilda Joubert	External independent consultant, partner in innovation at Synectics Europe, research associate in psychology, Open University.
Di Goldsmith	Former acting director of Arts Council East, advanced skills teacher, manager of the Oasis network of schools, Peterborough
Matt Reeve	Animator/film maker
Rosie Ward	Sound installation/artist
Gizella Warburton	Textiles/artist
VIEW 5	Artist company based in Peterborough
Anton Mirto	Performance artist
Chris Teasdale, Jan Williams	Installation artists

Timeline

Phase 1

May 2001	Fulbridge Junior School enters special measures
November 2001	Iain Erskine appointed head of Junior School
November 2001	Meeting with Roger Cole
May 2003	School comes out of special measures
September 2004	Iain Erskine appointed as head teacher of Fulbridge Primary School
September 2004	Fulbridge changes to become an all through primary

Phase 2

2006–7	CARA project[1]
2006–9	Di Goldsmith leads the Oasis initiative.[2] Mathilda worked with schools in the network and with staff, supporting in classrooms and staff meetings, including a professional day with other schools.

September 2009	Fulbridge becomes Creative Partnerships School of Creativity
January 2010	Enquiry project planning begins
May 2010	Start of enquiry project delivery
May 2010	School trips
June 2010	Mid-point evaluation
30 June 2010	Celebration of project
July 2010	Completion of project

The time to turn the ship around

Iain was clear from the start of this process that the change he sought would need a long time to see it through, and that it could not be achieved over the period of a few terms. Thinking about changes you would like to make in your school, do you see your school as something of an oil tanker, requiring several years to bring about the necessary change?

Or is it a faster, sleeker type of vessel which can adapt to change quickly?

On the other hand, is rapid change necessarily a good thing? Might there be advantages to taking a long period of time to institute a process of change?

Are there steps you would want to take to accelerate the process of repositioning your pupils at the centre of creative learning?

Early inspirations: Do you know a place that makes you long for childhood?

At the start of this process, I heard from educational adviser Roger Cole about a school in similar circumstances in Aylesbury which had developed a creative curriculum to lift itself out of its predicament. Roger's approach to developing our curriculum was based upon a question he asked of us as we showed him around our school: 'what place makes you long for childhood?' This provided the spur for me to develop a vision of how I wanted to lead Fulbridge Junior School in the future.

Roger suggested that children's learning schematas were not developed enough because of their lack of life experiences, whether these be things like going to the park, to the local woods or visiting the River Nene or other local sites such as Ferry Meadows.

Fulbridge's view of schemata[3]

Schemata are often referred to in the context of Piaget's work on child development. They describe the physical and mental actions involved in understanding and knowing and are sometimes viewed as categorical rules or scripts we use to interpret the world. In Piaget's view, a schema includes both a category of knowledge and the process of obtaining that knowledge. Fulbridge presents schema as being formulated on the basis of the life experiences that children have had:

Our schema interprets for us what others say or do, it is unique to us and determines our view of the world. As a consequence, the experiences that both parents and teachers give their children are of the utmost importance. The broader and more varied a person's experiences, the richer their own schema will be and so they will interpret and create in a more innovative way, their imagination will be more vivid. The more accurately children can observe, the more varied the skills they have and the more complete their mastery of them, so the more creative and imaginative they will be. If a life is lacking in experiences, then that person's schema will be an impoverished one and their imagination will have little or nothing to draw upon. At school we must compensate for the lack of experiences some children have had, through a carefully thought-out and experience-rich curriculum.

His approach to curriculum development was based on the concept of experiential learning, suggesting for instance that if children were studying the Second World War, then in order to learn about this time one would need to be fully immersed in it and experience it at first hand. Clearly, this was impractical, and so I was faced with the question of how close we could get to this scenario in the school in order to optimise the benefits of experiential learning that Roger was advocating.

FIGURE 1.1 School during wartime: preparing for defence

FIGURE 1.2 School during wartime: dress code of the times

Each year group tested this proposition through a series of pilot projects. In Year 6, for example, the school was temporarily redesigned as a school of the early 1940s. Children, staff and visitors were encouraged to dress up in clothes of the time, 1940s music was played in the corridors and public spaces of the school and there were other events which aimed to develop the feel of a school operating during wartime. But the big challenge came when Roger and I came up with a proposal which had the potential to create a series of shock waves throughout the school.

Visitors from a far, far, far away galaxy

We planned an event which we launched to the staff on the day before children were due to return to school from their Easter holidays. We had arranged for a large rock to be delivered onto the field, which would be presented to the children as a meteor. Beside it, inside a gazebo, an actor friend enacted the role of an injured alien. With a gas mask as protection and convenient disguise, I stood guard around the cordoned-off area to protect the children and parents as they arrived at school. Two scientists (role played by staff) wore white painting overalls and painting masks and two other staff were dressed as soldiers. The local policemen attended and the local newspaper sent a genuine reporter.

FIGURE 1.3 (above)
An alien has landed!
The scientists arrive

FIGURE 1.4 (left)
An alien has landed!
How to explain this?

FIGURE 1.5 An alien has landed! Keep the press away!

FIGURE 1.6 An alien has landed! Cordoning off the hazard

Staff brainstormed ideas as to how this event could be used, and decided that the alien was called Raba from Rabadoo, and lived on a pollution-free planet and ate and drank only healthy food.

They decided that he was very badly injured and his only hope of survival was to return to his planet. With the 'scientists' offering the school a million pounds for Raba, the children had to plan how to spend the money, and so they were presented with a moral dilemma to consider as well as issues relating to healthy eating and pollution. Other areas of the National Curriculum would fit into the follow-up work as the event evolved. Raba would be interviewed by the children, and written accounts and stories as well as artwork and research would follow.

Staff were, understandably, worried about the suddenness of the event, and pointed out that they had already planned the work they were going to do. But, with the subtext that if they wanted to see themselves as a creative school, the staff needed to be adaptable and innovative and prepared to take risks, Roger and I explained that if this incident had really happened they would not have been able just to ignore it.

The risk paid off: the children's enthusiasm and interest levels rocketed, with much writing and artwork being generated, as well as areas of enquiry in the science curriculum.

The sense of urgency to identify and prepare for a creative curriculum across the whole school – not just in one year group – at what would have been one of the school's busiest times of the year was potentially a very risky strategy. But with both the staff and governors' support, the teaching community at the school got behind the proposed new curriculum and we found ourselves at the beginning of a process which has continued since 2004.

This was the start of many such experiences that became the focal points of children's learning across the curriculum. We came to call them our 'truffle moments': special moments which supported children's learning.

Risking it: how far would you go?

Iain describes himself as a risk-tolerant individual and, together with his adviser, Roger Cole, presented staff with a hugely risky venture at the start of a new term: a new curriculum activity, little time to plan for it and unknowable outcomes.

How does your school respond to risk? Is it one where more time is spent on creating new learning opportunities or on cutting costs? Does your management team spend more time during meetings generating new ideas or discussing performance metrics? Do your school managers put off making a decision until only one option is still available?[4]

What might constitute a risk-tolerant or risk-averse culture in your school?

And are there staff members who are more inclined to risk than others? What characteristics do you think both these cultures show? And which ones would help promote creative learning in your school?

Extending the vision across the school

At the same time as this work, we also looked at nursery practice and decided that role-play areas were needed throughout the school: but role-play areas that were in line with the areas the children were studying. Egyptian, Tudor and Victorian areas were subsequently developed in the school, including a castle with a dungeon. My own office was found in the dungeon and I became a Dungeon Master rather than a Head Master; we created a Greek Agora in one of the corridors and a Post Office outside a classroom in another corridor; an Anderson shelter followed, as well as fairy-tale areas and book-based areas like Danny the Champion of the World. These areas were there to improve the learning environment, to make it a 'place that makes you long for childhood', and a stimulus for children's speaking and listening as well as their writing. Linking experiential learning to thematic areas of the school subsequently became the central focus of the school's approach to a creative curriculum.

The Peterborough Curriculum

In planning for long-term curriculum coverage, an essential question we asked ourselves was 'What has Peterborough got to offer?' We started listing local sites of interest, such as the cathedral, the museum, the river Nene, the local woods at Ferry Meadows and

FIGURE 1.7 On the way to the head teacher's office

FIGURE 1.8 (left)
What did Peterborough
have to offer in the past?

FIGURE 1.9 (below)
Transforming the school's public spaces

FIGURE 1.10 Transforming the school's public spaces

so on, attractions that were easily accessible to children. This allowed for the creation of themed topics that would address aspects of history, geography or science, with the necessary learning resources conveniently near at hand. We came to refer to this as our 'Peterborough Curriculum', and have found that if a curriculum can be developed from local, indigenous resources, then children are better equipped to contrast and understand more distant and abstract concepts such as the geography of far-away places, or the history of times long past.

We started with a geography or history focus of our own locality in the early years and then gradually widened this focus away from Peterborough as children grew older, whilst ensuring that their experiences further afield were understood within a context of understanding their own locality. The following are examples of how the 'Peterborough Curriculum' was developed across the school.

Year 2

Visit Stibbington Centre for a residential geography-based trip, including visits to the woods, a lake and conservation area. A topic based around the story of Shrek was developed which included a visit to natural areas that link to the environment Shrek lived in; we compared woodland animals in Shrek with local wildlife; children's writing focused on descriptive work about environments.

Year 3

The Invaders and Settlers topic is based around Flag Fenn. Geography work in school focuses on our locality to begin with, visiting local parks, the river, the Town Hall and the city centre, as well as touring the city and researching its history with respect to the railways, education and civic responsibilities. We visited the nearest seaside resort – Hunstanton – and children compared and contrasted environments as well as participating in beach studies and artwork connected to sea artefacts and then linking these activities to their writing, filming and photography.

Year 4

Amazing Africa focused on *The Lion King* and a visit to our local zoo, Whipsnade, and Hamerton. A camping trip to Edale in Derbyshire contrasted the Pennines with the Fens and Africa and gave the children the opportunity to walk up a large hill, go down a cavern and visit a castle whilst experiencing an environment that totally contrasted with their own.

Year 5

In studying the Tudors, pupils visited the grave of Catherine of Aragon in Peterborough Cathedral, and Fotheringhay church and castle. A medieval feast took place in the Tudor banquet corridor; the year group divided into poor and rich families and had to live in that environment throughout the week, designing their own menus and making pledges as to why they would provide society with a service or a product that would enable people to become rich. They also studied clothes and products used in Tudor times.

Year 6

Studies of the Second World War were given a Peterborough perspective. Pupils attended the Remembrance service in the city centre and met old soldiers from Peterborough. There was a visit to an Evacuee Day in nearby Stibbington village, which was used as an evacuee centre. Children assumed the identity of an actual evacuee for a day, using the Stibbington Education Centre. We also organised a visit to Ypres in Belgium and researched fallen Peterborough soldiers, in particular, the father of one of our governors.

Developing your own, vernacular curriculum

Have a look at the section on Vygotsky in the introduction to this book, which discusses how children understand the world through developing spontaneous concepts which are then transformed through language into scientific concepts. Also have a look at the section on Dewey in the introduction, which argues that education should be more orientated to children's lifeworlds, not only drawing on their own experiences, but also enabling them to participate more fully in a democratic society.

Iain and his staff developed a curriculum which was based on their own localities and which introduced children to the resources and funds of knowledge which those localities offered. This was fused with learning which emphasised the importance of experiential learning and enabled children to understand more distant and abstract concepts.

How influential is your school's locality in your curriculum? Can you identify how your locality might better inform your curriculum? How would you go about documenting the learning which arises from this type of work? Can you envisage a way in which children's engagement with your school's locality could enable them to participate more fully in their local communities?

What happened next?

I was aware that simply sending pupils out on trips did not constitute a full and progressive curriculum in itself. I was also conscious that whilst using Peterborough as a starting-point was useful, it could not be at the expense of areas of study that children needed to cover in order to prepare them for their secondary school curriculum. By aiming to make children's learning cross curricular we tried to ensure that their learning had a meaning, relevance and context. But we were aware that some areas of maths, for example, would not fit this ideal, and so we had to adopt a more pragmatic approach in addressing those curriculum demands.

For example, we teach mathematics each day for 45 minutes as well as having a 10-minute '4 rules' session (addition, subtraction, multiplication and division), and base our teaching on the interleaved and distributed principles.[5] One day a week focuses on 'Using and Applying', based on the topic theme when possible, and the other days are based on a two-week rota revolving around the following eight areas: weight and capacity (including calculations), money (including calculations), fractions, time (including calculations), length (including calculations), shape, number and data handling.

Fitting the maths square into the creative circle?

Would all maths teachers agree with Iain's assertion that maths cannot always have meaning, relevance and context?

We continued to develop a local, vernacular curriculum for the following five years. Whilst we started off almost as loners in the eyes of the local authority, connections with the QCA, the CARA programme run by CapeUK and work with Mathilda Joubert and the Oasis network of schools in Peterborough eventually led to our being identified as a Creative Partnerships School of Creativity in 2009.

Phase two of reforming our curriculum: moving towards a creative thinking skills approach

Becoming a School of Creativity (SoC) enabled us to begin to look at our curriculum with fresh eyes and focus on one specific area using the SoC template. It helped us to formulate new objectives for our reforming zeal and corresponded with a shift away from the focus on arts practice as a means to facilitating the curriculum and towards focusing more on developing children's creative thinking skills.

The strategic planning and delivery format provided by the SoC status meant that we had to work in a very different way to how we had worked before. We decided to focus on three lines of enquiry with a specific year group, beginning with discussions with each year group to identify their topics and key skills for the summer term. Once this had been achieved we identified where support was needed for pupils and teachers, what challenges we were facing and who could benefit from a creative project.

We decided to focus on Year 3, as this enabled us to create an ethos of learning with a year group that started school at the beginning of the creative journey and would be able to support other year groups in this process over the next few years. Our topic, Beside the Seaside, also provided an opportunity to use on-site locations to enhance writing through creative mediums and stimulus. The enquiry questions we developed through discussions with the year group and staff were:

1. How can we use external agents to support and encourage alternative structures to writing and motivation, whilst focusing on key skills?

2. How can we successfully explore curriculum links with writing through looking at specific mediums, such as sculpture, film, animation, drama?

3. How can we capture, explore and develop the senses, emotions and vocabulary experienced by our children during school trips?

We were particularly conscious that children's writing needed to improve and felt that if they were to write well, then they needed memories, an active imagination and experiences to draw upon. We wanted children to believe that they could write anywhere they were inspired to do so.

Refining the creative learning process: shifting from arts doing to creative thinking

Charlotte identifies a shift away from the focus on arts practice as a means to engaging children with the curriculum and towards focusing more on developing children's creative thinking skills. According to Bloom's Taxonomy,[6] creative thinking involves creating something new or original. It involves the skills of flexibility, originality, fluency, elaboration, brainstorming, modification, imagery, associative thinking, attribute listing, metaphorical thinking, making forced relationships. The aim of creative thinking is to stimulate curiosity and promote divergence.

What kinds of arts or other practice do you think you could use in your school to enhance children's thinking skills? What type of thinking skills might be best enhanced by different arts skills? You might find John Harland *et al.*'s *The Arts Education Interface: A Mutual Learning Triangle?* a useful source of information about how different art forms can benefit different learning styles and thinking skills.

Inspiring writing with creative practitioners' teams

To do this we employed several creative practitioners to participate in the school trip to Hunstanton seaside. Practitioners and children planned and explored ways of capturing the senses using film, photography, sketching, painting and words whilst at the beach, and then used that information to develop their writing back at school.

Each class paired up with two practitioners and worked through the processes of story writing, character description, poetry and persuasive writing using the practitioners' specific arts to stimulate writing and bring it alive.

In line with the school's themed corridor approach, we enhanced the school's environment by creating a beach, complete with caravan. The installation enabled children to display their work and discuss the process with friends, colleagues and family.

We wanted to have a museum feel and to allow classes to go back and explore the caravan area in their own time, as you would in a local museum. The caravan has been used by many year groups. Reception used the sand-pit and seaside area to develop gross motor skills, and Year 4 looked at it as a habitat. Year 1 explored the caravan to enhance its fairy-tale topic and Year 5 used it for maths investigations.

As we were keen to involve the whole school community in the project, we decided to recruit a group of mini-agents: about twenty pupils from across the school who were involved in the planning and interviewing processes, and attended the seaside trip to capture the responses and feelings of the children through photography, film and sound.

Practitioners, pupils and teachers worked together over seven days, exploring writing using different mediums. They used animation, movement, light and shadow, textiles, painting, sketching, etc. to stimulate and excite the children in writing about the seaside using different chosen genres. The external practitioners completed the teachers' and children's learning with a celebration day using the caravan gallery as the centrepiece.

What did the teachers learn from the process?

The real success of the project was the way in which creative skills were developed to capture, explore and develop the senses, emotions and vocabulary experienced by the children on their trip to Hunstanton, and this was evident in the tangible outcomes of the project (number 3 in list above).

Matters to consider: staff are doing it for themselves

An unexpected outcome of this process was that whilst staff had initially envisaged the creative practitioners providing the skills to explore alternative structures to writing, they unexpectedly found that the teachers had these skills themselves and that the role of the practitioners became to provide the necessary experiences to allow those skills to emerge and flourish.

For Charlotte and Iain, the value of the artists lay both in their expertise, language and techniques, and, more significantly, in bringing an outside perspective to the work they did with the teachers to broaden their critical thinking skills and to help the teachers to reflect more on their own considerable capabilities as creative practitioners.

'We've been doing this stuff for years', is another common observation heard from teachers interviewed for this book. How true for you is this statement? Have your creative skills been brought to the forefront or pushed to the sidelines of the classroom in recent years? How have you and your school's management team contributed or responded to that process?

Notes

1 Creative Partnerships initiated the Creativity Action Research Awards scheme (CARA) and CapeUK designed and ran the project during the school year 2004–5. The brief was to establish a partnership between a teacher and a creative practitioner and come up with an action research-based project that investigated an aspect of creativity. It was a national project, involving 104 individual projects running in 145 schools across the country. Nursery, primary, secondary and special schools were all involved and some networks of schools worked jointly in delivering their CARA project.

2 The Oasis Initiative was set up by Iain Erskine as an arts-based creative network to which 33 local schools signed up in order to share ideas and learn from each other.

3 http://www.fulbridgeschool.com/schoolcurriculumplan.htm.

4 See 'Project management for a risk averse culture', http://www.ehow.com/facts_6955204_project-management-risk-averse-culture.html#ixzz1HKc3Eaw8.

5 http://www.fulbridgeschool.com/schoolcurriculumplan.htm.

6 http://www.teachervision.fen.com/teaching-methods/curriculum-planning/2171.html.

Reference

Harland, J., Lord, P., Stott, A., Kinder, K., Lamont, E. and Ashworth, M. (2005). *The Arts-Education Interface: A Mutual Learning Triangle?* Slough: NFER.

2

Slow Bread, Slow Cities, Slow Pedagogy

Dale Primary School, Derby

Sarah Coxon

Editor's introduction

This case study demonstrates how immersive learning experiences can be engendered through adopting 'slow pedagogy'. This involves approaches to personalised learning which allow for:

- engagement in a curriculum which is driven by constant formative reflection;
- a profound knowledge of children's progression in skills; and
- learning which is fired by children's curiosity and questions.

Sarah Coxon, the year teacher who wrote this chapter, suggests, much like Iain at Fulbridge, that children's daily experiences provide them with limited opportunities for creative and cultural development. But, unlike Fulbridge, which relied on its immediate locality for inspiration, her school's solution for enhancing these experiences was galvanised by a study trip to the pre-schools of Pistoia in northern Italy.

Welcome to Dale Primary School!

Dale Primary is an inner-city school in Derby with a large and mixed staff – some who travel from a long distance and others who live in and know the community very well indeed. The local neighbourhood is composed mainly of Pakistani Muslims and a lot of the parents are from the Kashmir area of the Punjab, so there's quite a sense of village community in the area.

We thus have a high percentage of pupils from a Pakistani Muslim background. We are constantly striving to improve our standards but, because of our children's relatively limited life experience, we have to look for creative solutions which will both widen and enrich their education and improve basic skills. One of the big issues for the school is that often the community doesn't really recognise creativity, and so there are lots of problems related to getting children involved in aspects of school life. Dance and drama, for example, can be areas of school life in which parents don't want their children to participate.

Community values or community deficits?

Sarah suggests that there are parts of the local community who don't recognise creativity in the way that she expressed it. Why might this be a 'community' deficit? And what role should the school have in filling that deficit? Does your local community have similar 'deficits'? And to what extent is it up to the school to address those deficits?

Cast of characters/actors

Sarah Coxon	Year 6 teacher
Linda Sullivan	Head teacher
Paula Moss	Creative agent
muf	Architectural consultants
Dr Myra Barrs	Literacy consultant
Hannah Fox	Designer

Timeline

2006	Joined Creative Partnerships programme
February 2007	Trip to Pistoia
May 2007	Setting up of small development group of three teachers
September 2007	Setting up of research and development team
2009	Became a Creative Partnerships Change School Programme
	Piloting the Pistoia-influenced model in the classroom
	Year 4 example: The Antartica project
	Year 6 example: Getting back to our roots project

The developmental process

The impetus for radical change in our approach to the curriculum and learning environment at our school was an inspirational visit to nursery schools and children's centres in Pistoia, Tuscany, an Italian city with a child-centred ethos. I remember the website saying something like 'the entire city, as a place of life and culture, is at the service of children and constitutes a resource for their education'.

The Pistoia aesthetic

The pre-schools of Pistoia, Tuscany are renowned around the world for their innovative approach to early education. They have developed an approach to child development which identifies aesthetics as an essential factor in the organisation and acquisition of knowledge. Aesthetics, they suggest, are critical to learning and cognitive processes, and are not merely about making things look pretty.[1] The Pistoia aesthetic system has been described[2] as valuing:

1. Clarity and space;
2. Simplicity and continuity – white walls, limited colour, unity;
3. Simple, uncluttered graphic displays;
4. Transparent classification of objects and materials;
5. Effective colour relationships;
6. Displaying work done by children as 'exhibits';
7. Using a range and type of materials called 'Arte Povera' – poor materials transformed, found objects, plants, old electrical cables, etc.

We visited Pistoia in February 2007 as part of a larger group of teachers and head teachers which included our head and three members of Dale teaching staff. The visit grew out of our Creative Partnerships work with muf, an architectural art practice[3] that looked at the dynamic use of space. We had previously spent some time 'decluttering' spaces in school and were looking at alternative means of organising resources from an aesthetic point of view.

However, understanding of the value of an aesthetic approach – as exemplified by the Pistoia model – was not rooted in a coherent or collective vision for our school community. Recognising this, our creative agent, Paula Moss, came to us with an article about Pistoia, written by Dr Myra Barrs (Barrs, 2007), that opened our eyes to possibilities for real and sustainable change in our school. We decided to go and have a look for ourselves.

The visit was the catalyst for a radical shift in perspective for all involved. Here, in Pistoia, was a community of professional and experienced educationalists with a city-wide shared vision. It was a profoundly moving (and galvanising) experience to witness the real impact of an approach that was committed to:

- slow pedagogy, which allowed real time for children to learn, productively and profoundly;

- a curriculum driven by constant formative reflection (*real* personalised learning);

- the construction of learning in a community;

- a profound knowledge of children's progression in skills;

- learning fired by children's curiosity and questions;

- a strong aesthetic value system – a view that beauty breeds beauty;

- calm, organised learning spaces, allowing freedom;

FIGURE 2.1 A classroom before the Pistoia experience

FIGURE 2.2 Pistoia Piazza

- a meaningful immersion in the locality and environment;
- the entitlement of children to high-quality arts experiences;
- valuing teaching professionals for their intellect, strengths and passions;
- the involvement of professional designers in display documentation;
- multi-layered communication with parents and the wider community;
- the use of natural, recycled and found materials.

Points of drama during the first visit to Pistoia

The visit elicited profound emotional responses. We started before the trip thinking that we were just looking at learning environments, and whilst the teachers were quite happy to explore the aesthetic aspects of the schools we visited, the head teachers were somewhat intransigent to start with and insisted that the approach reflected a wider philosophy of teaching and learning. And yet, we were walking into schools that had a very potent visual arts base and were being overwhelmed by how beautiful everything in the buildings was. The heads responded along the lines of 'Oh yes, it's all very well but once you get the children actually involved – do the children actually touch any of these things?'

FIGURE 2.3 Pistoia school displays: 'Do the children actually touch any of these things?'

As we visited more than one school, we could see this shared aesthetic across the town. It was very orderly, very subtle, based around natural objects, very focused on muted colours, and we realised that there was far more to it, and that actually it was rooted in a very powerful ethos of children's curiosity-led learning: developing a community of learning and enquiry together, which was strongly embedded in the town of Pistoia, as was demonstrated in the stories of the children and their parents and their families.

Here was a realisation and a validation of all of those 'gut feelings' that a relevant, engaging and curiosity-led curriculum is what motivates, ignites and inspires our children to become life-long learners. We were given the confidence to start to reclaim our own curriculum and make it relevant to our needs as a community. We were also able to see at first hand how the aesthetic of a school impacted directly on the quality of learning. However much the potential barriers and worries loomed, we were all committed to using the experience as a vehicle for change.

When we returned to school, we knew we had to evolve – and we did. Linda, our head, led a staff meeting during the first week back in which all we did was show photos to the staff of the things that we had seen and talk about our emotional reactions. At the end of the staff meeting we had the same feeling that we had had on leaving Pistoia: we knew we had to change – but we didn't know how.

However, we did know that this was about giving trust back to teachers.

The next steps: spreading the message across the school

Subsequently, the three teachers who had been on the trip started to experiment in their classrooms with ideas and philosophies. We all documented our learning journeys, reflecting continually on our own practice and on the children's learning. We had to convince colleagues who had not experienced Pistoia at first hand that this was a relevant and purposeful way of working in Dale Primary.

One hurdle which became apparent was that some staff perceived those of us initially involved as 'creative' people. The challenge was how to sell the new approach to those who did not see themselves in this way. An INSET day introduced the key principles via a new approach to planning around a skills-based curriculum.

The 'creative individual' conundrum

Sarah points to a common experience that individual teachers are seen as 'more creative' than other members of staff. Sometimes, the presence of outside artists (or 'creatives' as they're sometimes unhelpfully called) can exacerbate this perception that some teachers are 'not creative': and this works to alienate those staff from the openings that the development of new learning opportunities presents to both teachers and pupils. Is this a common perception in your school? What does it mean in practice? How might you structure a CPD event to demonstrate that 'creativity' is present across the staff team? And that it doesn't rely on one simple set of technical skills, such as drawing?

Lesson plans

Eventually it became necessary to embark on a far more focused exploration of the 'Pistoia' way by widening the net beyond the three teachers' practice. It was at this point that we developed our relationship with Dr Myra Barrs as our new creative partner in guiding us towards a coherent, school-wide approach relevant to our needs.

A research and development team was established, with members of each year group as representatives, who would introduce the Pistoia way of working in their classrooms, as an initial step towards translating into good practice at Dale the themes that we had taken from Pistoia.

The research team worked either on a one-to-one basis with teachers, or with their year group teams to build further on the Pistoia experience so that we could define the key principles that should underpin our new creative curriculum and disseminate good practice to colleagues. We decided to focus specifically on the key theme of 'slow pedagogy'.

Our agreed definition of slow pedagogy was:

- a learner-centred pedagogy with a focus on what and how children learn, on their interests and strengths as learners, especially when their learning is self-directed;
- pedagogy that gives learning time: long-term projects that engage children and allow them to build up their understanding through revisiting and reworking ideas;
- reflective pedagogy, where planning and reflection are intertwined and where observations of children's learning informs teachers' planning.

The team's school-based enquiry was aimed at seeing what differences these changes in practice made to learners' learning and teachers' teaching. The focus questions for this research were:

- What changes in children's learning and achievement can be observed using this slow pedagogy approach?
- How did teachers' practice and thinking change when we adopted a slow pedagogy approach in the classroom?
- What structural and organisation changes would support teachers in adopting a slow pedagogy model?

We each kept detailed reflection logs to help us focus our responses, which recorded our trains of thoughts, reflections on our practice, and open structures for planning for possibilities, such as identifying stimulus, key skills, concepts and questions.

Slowness: an antidote to the fast society?

Slow pedagogy is echoed elsewhere around the world in the most interesting development: *Slow Cities, Slow Food and Slow Schools* are all part of a fascinating movement[4] to slow life down and to enable us to engage in deeper, more meaningful relationships and connections with the world. 'Slow pedagogy' is another manifestation of this movement. If you adopted this *slow pedagogy* approach in your school, what changes in children's learning and achievement might you see? Do you think these changes would be across the curriculum or in certain disciplines? How might the practice and thinking of your school's teachers change if you adopted this approach in the classroom? What structural and organisational changes in your school would support teachers in adopting a slow pedagogy model?

FIGURE 2.4 A space for slow pedagogy?

How do you know when you're witnessing creative learning?

Heightening teachers' powers of observation of creative learning

We focused on a few children to observe closely, using the Creative Learning Assessment framework to guide our observations. This framework was developed by Sue Ellis, Myra Barrs and Jane Bunting, researchers at the Centre for Literacy in Primary Education (CLPE) in collaboration with Lambeth Education Action Zone schools (Ellis *et al.*, 2007). It aims to provide teachers with a view of creative learning and development, a framework for observation-based assessment, and information to feed back into planning a creative curriculum which will be responsive to individual and group needs.

Making the learning visible

Graphic designer Hannah Fox worked alongside teachers at Dale to help us make the learning visible and to decide how to document learning processes and outcomes. As a team, we met several times throughout the year to reflect, to feed back findings and to discuss ways forward. Myra was instrumental in guiding us towards our own conclusions. She also provided an expert voice in the art of observation and reflection that we found invaluable.

At the end of the process, the research group devised a day of continuing professional development to disseminate its findings to the rest of the staff and for Linda to share her vision of the new Dale curriculum, incorporating four 'golden threads' as underpinning principles:

Giving Learning Depth
Learning for a Purpose
Reflection/Observation
Creativity and the Role of the Arts

We also developed a new planning framework (in use since September 2009), very much in line with the then new Rose report guidance on the curriculum (Rose, 2009), to help staff navigate their way around this new way of working and to focus us on planning possibilities rather than inevitabilities.

Using the Creative Learning Framework

Sue Ellis describes the CLA Creative Learning Continuum as providing a clear, informing and open structure for reflecting on progress (Figure 2.5).

Based on CLPE's Patterns of Learning continuum, it comprises:

(i)   confidence, independence and enjoyment;
(ii) collaboration and communication;
(iii) creativity;
(iv) strategies and skills;
(v)   knowledge and understanding;
(vi) reflection and evaluation.

The interdependent and non-hierarchical strands of the continuum form the key headings within the CLA observation framework which, together with examples, help to guide teacher observation and reflection on the creative learning process. They are not exhaustive, but indicative, and provide useful prompts for observation and analysis. Do you use a similar framework in your school to assess how creative learning is developing? How might you use or adapt this framework for your own purposes?

Teacher/TA	Year	Date	Date	Date
Name(s)				
Creative context				
(i) confidence, independence, enjoyment, e.g. developing pleasure and enjoyment engagement and focus empathy and emotional involvement self-motivation				
(ii) collaboration and communication, e.g. works effectively in a team contributes to discussion, makes suggestions listens and responds to others perseveres, overcomes problems communicates and presents ideas				
(iii) creativity, e.g. is imaginative and playful generates ideas, questions and makes connections risk-takes and experiments expresses own creative ideas using a range of artistic elements				
(iv) strategies and skills, e.g. identifies issues and explores options plans and develops a project demonstrates a growing range of artistic/creative skills uses appropriate subject specific skills with increasing control				

(v) knowledge and understanding, e.g.
 	
awareness of different forms, styles, artistic and cultural
    traditions, creative techniques
uses subject specific knowledge and language with
    understanding				

(vi) reflection and evaluation, e.g. responds to and comments on own and others' work responds to artistic/creative experiences analyses and constructively criticises work reviews and evaluates own progress				
Areas for further development				

FIGURE 2.5 The Creative Learning Assessment Framework

Implications for leadership and management

Without the bold leadership and vision of our head, Linda Sullivan, it would have been impossible for us to be so brave in our practice. The burden of accountability and the perceived conflict between a creative curriculum and a standards-raising agenda must not be underestimated.

As a staff, we had been given the green flag by our senior management team to be experimental. Linda, however, was putting her head above the parapet. Whilst she had the expert support of Myra as a sounding board, in implementing decisions for translating our vision of a Pistoia-style curriculum into practice and in keeping us on track, Linda is, of course, ultimately answerable to the powers that be. She had to convince our governing body of the value of this research model and she had to sort out the practicalities of releasing staff for meetings and reviews.

She also encouraged a sense of shared ownership and collective responsibility for the work by delegating responsibility to members of staff, which enabled them to become more autonomous. This meant that she also had a major role in reassuring staff during the process. The research not only left some of the team feeling vulnerable and isolated, working away from their year-group teams, but also had a similar impact on our colleagues. Planning in teams had largely disintegrated and it also became obvious that there were misconceptions about/negative views of the basis for this creative way of learning – primarily, that this was a return to 1970s-style, topic-based learning entirely led by children and with no basis in skills progression or teacher vision. Linda had to navigate a path to avoid 'us and them' tensions, keeping the channels of communication open.

In an age in which teachers have become increasingly corporate and deskilled through the prescriptive diet of QCA and SATs, it has been liberating to be given back the trust to do what we do best, to make judgements about the learning in our classrooms based on needs and our own strengths and interests.

The old chestnut: creativity in conflict with standards

Sarah suggests that one of the conflicts which affected the school's development process was the concern that an overemphasis on the creative nature of learning would conflict with the requirements to raise academic standards. This is a common refrain from many teachers who are anxious about the possible effects of refocusing their creative learning provision. But need they be mutually exclusive? Does your school perceive a conflict between a creative curriculum and a standards-raising agenda? And what reasons are given, if any, for this conflict?

What happened during the work?

During the initial work, immediately post-Pistoia, only the three teachers who had visited Italy trialled a new way of working. Each came off traditional timetabling and introduced topics around themes, in which all learning was sparked from an initial creative stimulus.

Instead of using normal school planning templates, teachers had an overview of outcomes and the progression of skills required, and planned for possibilities and challenges using the guidelines of the CLA framework. The weeks evolved, sometimes tangentially, in response to children's needs and developing lines of enquiry. As such, this involved daily re-evaluation and planning for next steps.

We began to look at the learning environment itself, and began to realise that the classroom environment was not very supportive of the learning that was happening.

Developing a plan

The topics that we were doing at that time of the year were nature-based topics with the overarching idea of getting back to our roots: asking questions about how we could bring nature into the classroom and how we take ourselves out into nature more often. We started to talk to Hannah Fox, with whom we had done a long project for our centenary book, and we decided that we couldn't carry on working as we were: we had to get our classrooms sorted before we could go any further. The children were asking 'How can we be doing a topic on getting back to nature when we can't see out of the window?'

Two examples of how we developed an approach in Years 4 and 6 are described below.

Piloting the Pistoia-influenced model in the classroom: Year 4 approaches

In Year 4, Jess Baird and her team colleagues used Antarctica as an overarching theme, with staff and pupils taking on the role of explorers in a 'mantle of the expert' approach. This was supported by a concurrent link to the Amundsen Omega 3 race to the South Pole.

Pupils planned, resourced and then carried out the expedition, which culminated in a 'Lonely Planet Guide' for Antarctica to showcase their learning. 'Ranulph Fiennes', corresponded almost daily with the children, setting them new tasks and challenges to help them to prepare for their mission. In the process of preparation, the children found out how to plot the most efficient routes; learned a variety of knot-tying techniques; made team flags; designed and made sledges, etc. Along the way, they couldn't help but learn about insulation or map reading or Antarctic habitats. The children were incredibly anxious not to miss any time off school because of their focus on the task.

Using real images of Antarctica, supplied by graphic designer Hannah Fox, the children were able to suspend reality and totally immerse themselves in the topic. Much of the time, the windows were thrown wide open, providing a suitably chilled atmosphere! One morning, their classroom became an aeroplane that transported them to Antarctica. Dressed up warmly, they set off in three teams in a race to the South Pole. The moment when they reached their destination was exhilarating! The children exclaimed that they thought they would never get there, but managed it because they worked as a team: 'no-one was left behind'! There was a genuine sense of collective achievement.

FIGURE 2.6 The start of the exploration of Antarctica

FIGURE 2.7 No one left behind!

The power of context in this case was immense, and the collaborative skills as well as knowledge and understanding that came out of it were staggering. Moreover, the sense of it being real was conveyed to parents. One mother came to the Year 4 teachers concerned about being able to afford the fare to Antarctica!

The experiential aspect of the work meant that children entered willingly and enthusiastically into the production of the 'Lonely Planet Guide'. The writing seemed to flow effortlessly; they knew what they were talking about.

Following the topic, children were invited to visit another local school to talk to the children in their role as explorers who had visited the South Pole. Staff were amazed by the children's subject knowledge and confidence. Also, at the very end of the topic, there was even an awards ceremony, with 'Ranulph Fiennes' presenting certificates to the children! Everyone knew it was really Mr Harris, but nobody let on!

There were parents who attended the presentation and we heard some of them saying 'We never did this when I was at school'. They really got involved in the topic.

Piloting the Pistoia-influenced model in the classroom: Year 6 approaches

In Year 6, the topic was entitled Getting Back to Our Roots, a nature-based project inspired by our children's lack of 'outdoor' experience. The topic was mainly focused on trees and started with a sensory stimulus through a winter's-day visit to the local park. Here, children went on canopy walks, blindfolded each other and hugged trees,

FIGURE 2.8 'We never did this when I was at school!'

FIGURE 2.9 Getting back to our roots

worked out non-standard measures of tree girths and heights, collected seed pods and twigs, did bark rubbings, observed animal habitats, and looked closely for faces in the peeling bark of London planes.

This then stimulated a number of questions and lines of enquiry that the children themselves identified. They very quickly wanted to know about the inner workings of trees and through drama and active research activities were able to explore the functions and parts of trees to a high level. It was fantastic to see children who may have been previously identified as the special needs children absorbed into the community of learning and quite confident with their use of high-level concepts and terminology relating to the cambium, phloem and xylem. This may not have been KS2 curriculum material, but it was the depth to which the children were willing take their own learning.

The children began to produce work of a far higher quality: observational sketches, collage, sculpture, explanatory texts, mathematical investigations into calculating the age of trees. All flowed quite naturally from their innate enthusiasm – a real case for purposeful learning.

The high quality of the work that the children produced and the desire to display and celebrate it took them on an unexpected tangent. The graphic designer commented on how the work seemed to get lost amongst the primary-coloured paint and target-based wallpaper. When we explored this with the children, they were very clear that they didn't take much notice of the visual resources around the room, the washing-line reminders and targets. Their overall feeling was of clutter and being cramped and overwhelmed, not of an atmosphere conducive to learning. One child even commented:

'Why have we got blinds at the windows when we want to be bringing nature into the classroom? We can't see outside!'

Radical action was taken and, with the permission and support of parents and families, the children reclaimed their learning environment, getting rid of unnecessary clutter, painting the room magnolia, removing blinds and replacing them with white muslin curtains, rearranging their space. The new sense of space and light precluded plastering the walls with resources again. Instead, only high-quality stimulus materials (e.g. images of Alice Oswald's poems or David Nash's sculptures), natural objects for exploration (seed pods, bark, pieces of wood, leaves) and examples of the children's work were displayed. Resources were organised clearly and beautifully, colour coordinated and tidy. The children started to take far greater responsibility for caring for their space because of their dramatic sense of ownership.

The principles of the Pistoia aesthetic finally made sense in practice.

What the work achieved

Most powerful for the teaching staff was a renewed self-belief in themselves as educators and professionals. Our increasingly focused observation and reflection of children allowed us to really meet the needs of our pupils. There was an initial sense of guilt, particularly in KS2, about not always being involved in direct teaching. However, it soon became apparent that the scheduled observation of the children was a far more powerful tool in moving them forward, as well as taking the learning deeper.

FIGURE 2.10 A classroom after the Pistoia experience

FIGURE 2.11 The results of children taking care over their learning spaces

FIGURE 2.12 (below) Decluttered classrooms

The cross-curricular nature of the work allowed us to provide meaningful opportunities for children to apply newly acquired skills in a range of contexts. It particularly provided 'pain-free' opportunities for the children to write.

Whilst still acting as teachers, mentors and guides, we were able to facilitate far more independent learning. Children started to take greater responsibility for their learning and took on a role in constructing their own learning. We felt liberated by allowing children to make choices and planning only for possibilities rather than pre-ordaining learning outcomes. The Year 5 teacher, Karen Ratcliff, relished the opportunity to move away from the restrictive, unit-based approach, e.g. *This half term we are doing Tudors and this is what and how we will learn.* One child in Year 6 made the profound and shocking observation that 'You are no longer spoon-feeding us!'

In our children, we witnessed:

- a far greater sense of engagement and motivation;
- an increased willingness to take risks and embark on challenges;
- more resilience and perseverance, on account of the emotional investment in what they were doing;
- sustained periods of high-quality work;
- a sense of achievement, pride and success;
- subject knowledge which moved way beyond the expectation of the year group; and
- increased levels of questioning and higher-order thinking skills.

The children have also learned to become more reflective, showing an increased awareness of their own strengths and weaknesess and what next steps they need to take in their learning. They have become increasingly able to reflect on their learning, and in doing so have developed a high level of learning vocabulary.

A conversation with the school improvement partner (SIP)

We had our SIP (school improvement partner) come to visit us. He had come on one of his fact-finding missions for the authority and he needed to have a look around school to check our school environment and he was checking that we had the 'correct' learning environment, that we had our targets and our objectives on the wall, and so on.

I took him into one classroom and the targets and objectives were up on the wall and he was impressed, but I said to him that he wouldn't find that in every classroom and I took him into Sarah's room. There were photographs and poems on the wall and he walked in and he just said 'There are no targets here!'

I said that the children wanted this kind of environment and I explained how they had painted the classroom. I told the children that Mr Arthur had come to see how we worked and whether we'd got the right things in our classroom and that he was a bit concerned because we had no targets on the wall. Sehrene said: 'Well, we used to have those on the wall but we don't have them now because it just used to fill up our minds with clutter . . . they're in our heads. Why do we need them on the wall?'

> Then the children explained that they had changed their room because before it hadn't allowed them to think, and now they were able to think and they were able to be calm. So the children were our best ambassadors.

In terms of relationships, there was an increased team spirit and bond between pupils and teacher and, particularly, between pupils. There was a genuine sense of belonging to a learning community in which we all supported each other's journeys. Teachers were no longer the font of all knowledge, with the children as empty vessels. To see traditionally non-academic children excel was particularly rewarding. Collaborative skills improved hugely, with an ethos of support and encouragement coming to the fore.

Difficulties in the journey

During the research process, we encountered many hurdles. In Year 6, some children just didn't seem to respond well to this way of learning. They appeared passive and uncooperative. However, in closely observing their behaviours it became obvious that their micro-steps were as significant as, if not more so than, the leaps and bounds being made by others. Sometimes as teachers we make misplaced assumptions based on outcome rather than process.

In Year 5, the teacher found that her more able children really struggled with the lack of traditional structure. In this way of working, no one dominant voice was accepted. Some of the gifted and talented children, again in close observation, exposed their insecurities about risk-taking. Learning through mistakes – and there were many – was not a route they were comfortable with.

Labelling children: looking out for the deficits

Sarah suggested earlier on that this new approach to learning was having a noticeable impact on how children – particularly those labelled as 'special needs' were achieving. Here too, in the Year 5 class, the 'gifted and talented' children are also seen to be responding to the challenges of the work in an unexpected fashion.

Is there something about this kind of teaching and learning that requires us to redefine what we mean by 'special needs' and what we mean by 'gifted and talented'? How does placing students at the heart of creative learning change our knowledge and perceptions of what they may or may not be capable of?

The four golden threads of the creative curriculum

As the whole school has adopted the new creative curriculum with its 'four golden threads' – learning depth, learning for a purpose, creative in the arts and reflection – we have now become far more flexible in our approach to planning and learning. Topic

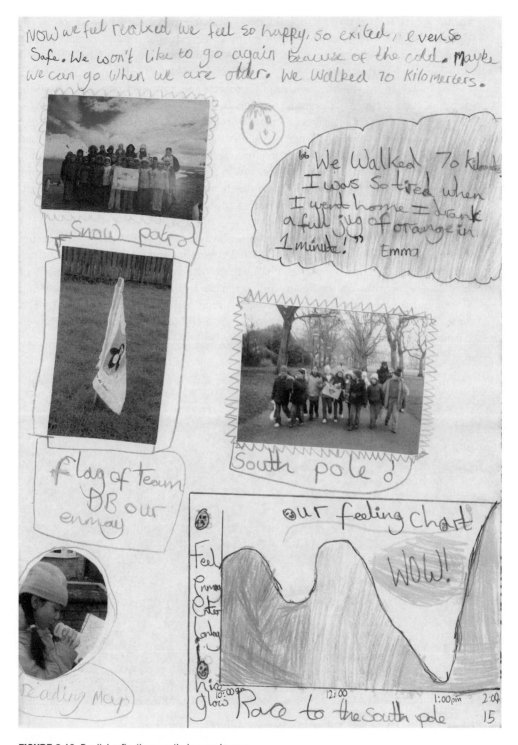

FIGURE 2.13 Pupils' reflections on their experiences

themes are established with a strong skills-base underpinning them. These topics are not rigid and allow for more child-directed learning. Time is also not a constraint. Topics come to a natural end, at the point at which children's learning has delved deep and broadly into the subject area.

We are seeing big differences in pupils' progress and learning aptitude as a result of our new curriculum. As teaching professionals, we have learned to take a step back. Observing children on task gives us a far better 'whole child' perspective, and reflecting on their learning and our own practice allows us to provide meaningful, personalised learning. The children have also become more articulate in discussing their learning.

We have learned not to limit the horizons in learning. Coverage is often the enemy of learning, and our focus has shifted to depth and breadth of experience rather than skimming the surface. As a result, children's knowledge and understanding way exceeds expectations.

From the Year 6 research, we have finally found a relevance and ownership of learning environment. As a result, we have redecorated classrooms and corridors, stripped them back and created a sense of order and balance, and also a shared aesthetic. Our resident graphic designer oversees the documentation materials that communicate, both within school and to the wider community, what learning has taken place. The quality and aesthetic of this display material has raised our game and our expectations. It is all about having courage in your convictions.

FIGURE 2.14 Experiencing the results of the four golden threads of the curriculum

Matters to consider: new beliefs, new skills, new learners

Whilst on one level Fulbridge and Dale look like they took radically different steps in developing curricula which placed their children at the centre of creative learning processes, their destinations have covered some common ground:

- There has been a shared, renewed sense of self belief by teachers in their abilities.
- Cross-curricular working has provided meaningful opportunities for children to learn, and particularly to develop their skills in writing.
- Children have developed a greater ability to work as independent learners.
- Cross-curricular topics are taught, but with a strong underpinning of skills development.
- Depth and breadth of experience have replaced the urge for curriculum coverage.
- The quality of the aesthetics of the learning environment plays a significant role in enhancing the learning experience.

Vernacular or global: where to begin?

If Fulbridge and Dale represent two ends of a spectrum for recentring children at the heart of the creative learning experience (either starting in the local – Fulbridge, or starting in the global – Dale), where does your school fit on this spectrum?

Would it benefit your children if you were to able to offer more opportunities to learn about what's on their local doorsteps?

Or would it be of more benefit to cast your nets wider and look at practices further afield?

FIGURE 2.15 Placing students at the centre: starting with the local or the global?

Notes

1 For more on theories of aesthetic learning, see Woods, P. (1993) 'Towards a theory of aesthetic learning', *Educational Studies*, 19(3): 323–38.
2 http://www.whatchildrenmakeofthings.co.uk/pistoia.html.
3 http://www.muf.co.uk/.
4 http://www.slowmovement.com/.

References

Barrs, M. (2007) 'The creative community of Pistoia', *Teaching, Thinking and Creativity*, 22.

Ellis, S., Barrs, M. and Bunting, J. (2007) *Assessing Communication and Learning in Creative Contexts*, London: CLPE/CfBT.

Rose, J. (2009) *Independent Review of the Primary Curriculum: Final Report*, London: DCSF Publications.

Woods, P. (1993) 'Towards a theory of aesthetic learning', *Educational Studies*, 19(3): 323–38.

3

Pulling the Rug Out from Under Our Feet

Old Park Primary School, Telford

Mandie Heywood

Editor's introduction

In this chapter, 'real world' learning is demonstrated by Old Park Primary School in Telford and its focus on Learning to Learn (L2L) strategies and how these connect with the work of Guy Claxton's Building Learning Power programme as part of the school's bigger commitment to the Personalised Learning Agenda.

The gateways to personalised learning that this school has developed in order to make sure that bespoke or 'tailored' schooling is suitable to their particular community and student population are:

- learning to learn;
- curriculum characterised by deep learning, cross-curriculum activities and flexible timetabling;
- school design and organisation (Sanders, 2010);
- workforce development, particularly through an approach which the head teacher characterises as 'pulling the rug out from under their feet': an approach which offers new insights into how to continually galvanise change in a school whilst simultaneously keeping the staff on board.

Fulbridge, Dale and Old Park all offer different responses to the challenges provided by the resources of the outside world. Whilst Fulbridge sees value in its local resources, with its explicit valuing of Peterborough, and Dale travels over 1,000 miles to value the approaches of an Italian pre-school system, the head at Old Park Primary, Mandie Heywood, sees local culture as having little to offer in terms of cultural stimulus and expects her school to provide learning experiences which she suggests are not available in the wider community. The chapter is written by the editor from transcribed interviews with Mandie.

Old Park Primary School: three schools into one will go?

Old Park Primary School is based in Telford and is the result of a combination of two amalgamations. In 2004, an infants' school and a junior school occupied the same site and I was charged with amalgamating both schools into a new one: Langley St Leonard's Primary School. The process of amalgamation continued in 2007, when another local primary school was added to the duo, and in November 2008 this new amalgam of three schools moved to a new site which had a capacity for over 600 children (including a sixty-place nursery) – a relatively large primary school by most standards.

The school is located in Malinslee, an area of the town with a higher-than-average proportion of social housing. I was told when I first arrived here that before the collapse in the housing market the housing would have cost more to rebuild than it was worth on the open market, so it's quite a poor area. Forty per cent of our children have free school meals and we have a large number of children with special needs and we have a large number of looked after children as well. But we're pretty much a white working-class population. At last count about 50–60 per cent of our parents had no educational qualifications whatsoever and only about 40 per cent had cars.

I think these influences motivate teachers to raise aspirations, to give children a wider and deeper view and understanding of the world they live in and to encourage them to dream and aspire for a livelihood beyond their everyday experiences.

FIGURE 3.1 Old Park Primary School playground

Signs of social poverty? Or unseen funds of local knowledge?

Mandie's suggestion that the school's local communities are somehow impoverished and that children don't get access to the cultural experiences that they should is often heard from many schools in similar contexts. Might there be a danger that indicators such as free school meals, special needs, car ownership and parental qualifications negatively bias our perception of our children's backgrounds? How 'impoverished' is the area in which your school is based? What are your definitions of educational poverty? And are there links here with the labelling of 'deficit communities' as referred to in the previous chapter?

Are there perhaps other ways of interpreting what a local school's community does offer, as opposed to what it doesn't? What effect might this perceived impoverishment have upon a school's intentions to place pupils at the heart of the learning process?

FIGURE 3.2 Signs of social poverty? Or unseen funds of local knowledge?

Cast of characters and their roles in innovating the curriculum

Mandie Heywood, head teacher	Instigator, vision holder, follower through, holder of principles
Sarah Machin, deputy head	Translator of vision to existing staff
Julie Bebb, assistant head, SENCO	Designer
(Name not known), arts co-ordinator	Implementer

John Cocker, creative arts team,   Funder
Telford Arts
Richard Shrewsbury, creative agent,   Broker with artists and external partners
Creative Partnerships

Whilst there are certain key personnel involved in the process, everybody's been involved all the way through. You can't do this alone: you can lead and say 'This is where I think you ought to go', but unless you've got everybody as part of the process, you won't get anywhere. I was very fortunate in that the assistant head was my previous deputy and I managed to bring her over here. She knew the kind of things I liked to happen.

But, all the way through, we have had to keep coming back, revisiting and asking 'What difference has that made? How have we done that? Can we share practice amongst us? Can we go and look for practice outside school?' An awful lot of it has grown from people going outside school – and often that's me – and coming back and saying 'I've got a really good idea for you', but then developing it in our own way.

Timeline

November 2002	Started working with Creative Partnerships
September 2004	First amalgamation
Summer 2005	Restaurant project
Autumn 2005	Museum project
Summer 2006	Work on curriculum and consultation on second amalgamation
Autumn 2006	Two staff started to work together on curriculum projects
September 2007	Second amalgamation and introduction of Building Learning Power
December 2007	Business fair
Summer 2008	Finalised curriculum
April 2009	Applied to CCE for Creative Partnerships School of Creativity (SoC) status
January 2010	Launch event of SoC status

What does a creative curriculum mean to you?

I joined the school in 2004 and oversaw the joining together of three schools in my early days as head. The importance of a creative curriculum was clear from our first amalgamation because of the history of the two schools. They were very National Curriculum and QCA based and we had a lot of difficulties: we had a lot of children with challenging behavioural problems and I felt that we needed to completely transform learning. We weren't going to raise standards unless we made the children want to come to school.

I've never been a lover of QCA at the best of times. I quite like to have ceremonial burnings of it if I can. So the stimulus to develop a creative curriculum was, crucially, about the engagement of pupils. I strongly believe that doing more and more of the same is not going to raise standards, so you have to do something different.

FIGURE 3.3 Doing business at Old Park Primary School

The ethos of the old school was very controlled and oppressive. I did spend one term in the school prior to taking on the headship and it was a horrible place to be. The children were very, very controlled. The teaching was mediocre because there was a view that if you don't buy into what we do, then that's your problem.

So we needed to change the whole ethos and put people at the centre of everything, and we had to modify curriculum for some children who were struggling – but we needed to engage children and make them want to be here. We needed to give them some ownership of their learning; give them some feeling of control over what was happening. So that was really the root of our work and we've gone on from there and want our curriculum to be interesting and engaging for everybody.

The National Curriculum, QCA guidelines[1] and other contemporary educational horror stories

In this context, Mandie refers to the National Curriculum and QCA as providing straitjackets which teachers were expected to don without questioning or resistance. Although she does not explain why these frameworks became so limiting, she does suggest that they are the main forces for why teachers have lost ownership of their teaching. But is this necessarily true?

Do you have examples where the QCA guidelines have been used as just that – guidelines, rather than strictures?

What counts for you as a source of authoritative text or inspiration?

The ceremonial burning of QCA guidelines might also provoke a cheer amongst many teachers who have felt restricted by their existence: but is there a danger, in that process of rejection, that some useful, constructive ways of placing students at the heart of creative learning could be missed?

Burning the QCA guidelines

I don't like a curriculum where the children do the same thing year in and year out because I think that's very stifling for everybody and very boring. What kind of excitement is there for children if you know that when you get to Year 4 you are going to make a sandwich? I know QCA was never designed to be used like that, but that's how it's often used. There's been a view that if we're covering QCA, then we're covering the curriculum and we're OK. Well, I don't agree.

So when I first came here the aim was to try to create a curriculum that was much more relevant to our children, much more inspiring and engaging; and, wherever

FIGURE 3.4 Feeding 120 local people

possible, to have a real context for learning. In the very first year I introduced quite a big project working alongside the Telford Arts team, just as a way of demonstrating that something like this is possible. We ran a restaurant and Year 5 were involved with that project for a term. I involved two teachers: one was the arts coordinator and the other was one who happened to be working in the same year group, who I thought was going to be my biggest critic. Every single child was involved; we opened the restaurant on two evenings and we fed over a 120 people. And that critical teacher said at the end that it was the best thing that she'd ever done in all of her 20 years of teaching!

'Real world' learning: what exactly does that mean?

Mandie suggests that if learning takes place in a 'real world' context it can have greater value than a classroom-based curriculum. For Mandie, this means teaching content that is not arbitrary, but set in a context in which pupils can see the purpose behind it. And the meaning of 'real world'? In this instance, the 'real world' can mean the economic world of what it is like to run a restaurant, organising tea dances in Year 4, providing a Taste of India day with parents, running a Wild West Rodeo day, a Lighthouse day with parents, Taiko Drumming, Knight and Armour workshops, Lego workshops, a Pirate week and ending half a term's work about Shakespeare with Year 1 pupils with a performance of a version of *The Tempest*.

The 'real world', in Old Park's sense, allows for all sorts of possibilities for learning. What might 'real world' learning mean to you in your school? How significant could it be in placing your children at the centre of their learning experiences?

The first example of innovation: feeding the local world

The first project I introduced to the school was to set up a project with the local arts agency, Telford Arts, based on developing a school restaurant. The project involved the children in:

- visiting restaurants and hotels, where the chefs would show them what to do, followed up by more hands-on experience when they were back in school;
- working with chefs and cooks – seeing how a restaurant kitchen works, working with chefs in school to develop dishes to go on a menu, and doing market research about likes and dislikes;
- working with the environmental health officer on food hygiene;
- producing menus/leaflets/flyers;
- writing job descriptions and applying for the jobs they wanted. When they were allocated jobs, they worked with different people in a training format – all as either waiters or waitresses;
- working out budgets and costing the menu;

FIGURE 3.5 Heaven is a plate on earth

■ working with a visual artist to transform the hall into a rain forest in which the restaurant would be based. They used the Rain Forest café in London as a model and one pupil named the restaurant Heaven Is a Plate on Earth.

First steps and first difficulties

This was not a simple process though: I faced some critical opposition from one teacher who had been working in the school for over 20 years. So I invited the deputy head from my previous school to come and talk to those teachers who were particularly anxious. She brought copies of her own school's term plan, and demonstrated how it had achieved its project, which had the effect of reassuring and inspiring teachers – whilst not giving them a model to work to either.

In order to secure funding, I also had to ensure buy-in from John Cocker of the creative arts team at Telford Arts, who was able to point to a funding source which would enable the proposed project to take shape. He was central to the success of the restaurant project, finding the right professionals for the job in addition to the necessary funding.

Finding new funding from ever-shrinking sources

John's support during the fund-raising process meant that he was able to work with staff for a whole term before any curriculum activity took place. He also ensured that some initial catalytic funding of a few thousand pounds was in place in order to test the validity of the idea that Mandie had proposed. How might you start new initiatives in times of shrinking budgets? Can you identify where different funding sources might be in your school's locality?

Spreading the message across the school

The fact that I was new to the school afforded me the opportunity to push some boundaries that might have been more resistant to change, had I been more established in the school. The school sceptics may have been disinclined to say 'no' to this initiative, but, to their credit, they were prepared to follow the idea. Once the success of the restaurant had been established, I was able to use it as a springboard to look at the whole curriculum across the entire school.

I tried to introduce the little things along the way of which everybody had some experience. I like to add in 'pull the rug out moments', as the staff like to call them, where I'll go into a staff meeting and say 'OK, well this is what we're going to do' and they all go 'Ohhhhh!' We did a museum week and they had to work with the children and not decide what they were going to do in advance. But out of the void created by the pulling the rug out moment some creativity arose and people said 'That was great – that was a brilliant event'.

Faith, idiosyncrasy and orthodoxy

Mandie's 'pulling the rug out' moments reflect her approach to stimulating radical change in her staff and developing a climate which is used to experiencing sudden shocks in order to generate creative learning opportunities for staff and pupils. Using acts of faith and belief to structure an educational approach is certainly not new. Dewey in his paper 'My pedagogic creed' (Dewey, 1897), also asserts many statements of belief as to what constitutes an essential education. What would you say is your 'pedagogic creed'? And how does it inform how you place your students at the heart of the creative learning process?

We used those two events as a springboard for looking at the curriculum, and we said 'What could we do about our curriculum to make it more engaging?' So we spent quite a lot of time, as a whole staff, looking at the National Curriculum and stripping out all of the content aspects – any of the knowledge we kind of got rid of – and looking at what the skills were. I believe that we don't all have to study the same four periods

FIGURE 3.6 A successful restaurant leads to a review of the whole curriculum

of history in order to be rounded human beings by the time we get to later life, and it really doesn't matter what historical context you choose so long as you've got some progression and skills. So eventually we looked at all of the curriculum areas, stripped out everything and ended up with a skills progression.

Knowledge or skills?

Mandie articulates particularly clearly her belief that subject knowledge is subservient to the bigger task of progressively building skills. How far would you go in prioritising skills and their progression over knowledge? What babies are thrown out with this particular bathwater?

Creating an engaging curriculum: making an assault on the National Curriculum

This became the foundation for rebuilding a curriculum for children in Key Stage 2 which was specific to Old Park. The framework of skills was described under seven headings:

- creativity;
- IT;
- communication;
- problem solving;
- cross-curricular links;
- independent learning;
- Building Learning Power.

I was conscious too that this development was being undertaken nationally with the parallel promotion of the Personal Learning and Thinking Skills (PLTS) agenda.[2] I was also aware that this agenda had been promoted in the first phase of the school amalgamation, but I didn't want to risk a perception of one school's being taken over by another in the second amalgamation, and so I wanted something new for the new staff. I subsequently introduced Guy Claxton's Building Learning Power programme into the discussions of stripping the curriculum of its content and simultaneously building the new skills framework.

What is Building Learning Power?

Building Learning Power™ (BLP) is an educational programme developed by Guy Claxton and promoted by The Learning Organisation which claims to address deep learning in schools. The BLP programme has been introduced in secondary and primary schools across the country with the intention to improve student demeanour, behaviour and attainment. It is based on the premise that learners have 'learning muscles' and that there are four dispositions – the 4 Rs – which build up these muscles: resilience, resourcefulness, reflectiveness and reciprocity.

One consequence of this approach has been that the children themselves are now much more likely to be involved in developing their own curriculum – and there are mechanisms in the school to allow for their voices to be aired, shared and acted upon. An example of how we have translated these programmes into a particular work plan is attached below. The worksheet demonstrates how a theme, 'Contrasting UK locality: Church Stretton', can be translated into the skills frameworks we are using.

Lesson plans: sample of Autumn 2008 project

Subject: Geography major topic, Year 5/6

Creativity	Cross-curricular links	ICT	BLP collaboration	Speaking and listening	Problem solving	Independent learning/study skills
• I write poetry, newspaper reports, e-mails, persuasive letters, etc. about places, weather, geographical features studied. • I draw a variety of thematic maps based on own data. *Activities:* • Write emails • River poems	• I use charts, graphs and map overlays. • I present findings graphically. • I use 8 compass points confidently and accurately. • I use 4-figure coordinates confidently to locate features on a map. • I begin to use 6-figure grid refs; use latitude and longitude on atlas maps.	• I make a judgement about the best angle or viewpoint. • I use photos for investigations. • I evaluate the usefulness of recordings and the quality of the evidence collected. • I use a digital camera, video and sound recording. • I import photographs, video and sound clips into other programs – Photo Story. • I use a scanner or digital camera to create images for use in design. • I use multimedia packages, download from file/internet images, sound, video to create presentations.	*Activities:* • Capitalising – Local research, pose question pre-visit • Who will have info? How can they use each other best. Adult support. P29 • Collaboration • Work in groups to find information • Planning – plan visit	• I use appropriate language. • I evaluate the quality of the evidence collected. • I use appropriate vocabulary to communicate findings.	• I suggest questions for investigation. • I analyse evidence and draw conclusions, e.g. compare historical maps of varying scales; compare temperature of various locations and influence on people/ everyday life; use field work data on land use to compare land use/ temperatures, look at patterns and explain reasons behind them. • I use/recognise OS map symbols. • I use atlas symbols.	• I use primary and secondary sources of evidence in investigations. • I investigate places with more emphasis on the larger scale, contrasting and distant places. • I collect and record evidence unaided. • I find/recognise places on maps of different scales (e.g. River Nile). • I draw/use maps and plans at a range of scales. • I confidently identify significant places and environments as stated within KS2 National

- I use the features of programs and a variety of media to create suitable presentations for particular audiences, e.g. using PowerPoint.
- I use e-mail to contact others to share information and ideas – set up link with primary school in Stretton.

- I compare maps with aerial photographs.
- I select a map for a specific purpose (e.g. pick atlas to find Taiwan, OS map to find local village).
- I use atlases to find out about other features of places (e.g. find wettest part of the world, mountain regions, weather patterns).
- I describe features shown on OS map.
- I locate places on a world map.
- I draw a plan view map accurately.
- I use index and contents page within atlases.
- I use OS maps.
- I confidently use an atlas.
- I recognise world map as a flattened globe.

- Curriculum.
- I begin to identify places and environ-ments on maps within KS3 National Curriculum (see www.nc.uk.net//nc/contents/geog.htm for maps).

Assignments:
- Present a range of maps – major towns, physical, rivers, places of interest, population
- Fact file of Church Stretton
- River study

> ## Interrogating the translation of a geography topic into the skills orthodoxy
>
> The table shows how the school has translated a major geography topic in Years 5 and 6 into a collection of skills and activities pupils supposedly will engage with through the school's skills framework. How would you adapt this model to teaching geography in your school? Would this be a useful approach in other subjects, such as history, languages or maths? What is missing from this model? How would you assess pupils' achievement in this framework? And would some skills be more 'important' than others? How would you teach so as to develop these skills? And how would you be able to map a progression from the previous year and provide evidence for Year 7 teachers (for example) that pupils had achieved a suitable standard to be able to cope with the rigours of secondary education?

Critical spaces

The second amalgamation, between the three schools, entailed the building of an entirely new building – something I was determined to make sure I was able to influence from the beginning.

We wanted a building that had a heart – something in the middle that nobody felt they were miles away from. This building is huge: the capacity is for 560 children plus a 60-place nursery. We're not that big yet, but the authority built it because of the housing in the area, so that was the necessary size.

But we didn't want it to feel like a huge dinosaur of a building, and so wherever a child was they should never feel that they were too far from the centre. Their circulation area is relatively small and even though they will go to all parts of the building they shouldn't feel that it is miles to go. There are no spaces for one person – all the spaces are shared. I share with the deputy, and the assistant head works there when she's not teaching. So there is no room that is the domain of one person.

This is because if no one is there, then it becomes a dead space. Every space must be able to be used for children all of the time. So there are no names on doors. We've got an inclusion centre built in because we've always provided nurture groups, but we also have a team that works with very challenging children and they have to be able to get around the building quite quickly.

Where to now?

Old Park Primary is a school of dynamic teachers who independently look for creative opportunities in their classroom. They're now happy to push the boundaries themselves, although they haven't as yet pulled the rug out from under my feet! But I do now get staff coming to me with tentative ideas, saying 'Well, what do you reckon?' There is now less of a sense of staff asking, 'Well, what is she going to hit us with next?' and more of a feeling that staff are more comfortable with taking risks and allowing children to take the lead in learning.

FIGURE 3.7 Where to next?

Matters for consideration: Whose rug? Whose feet?

When she arrived at the school in 2004, Mandie had an initial opportunity to appoint four younger teachers, but since then has been unable to make any further staff appointments because the amalgamations affected her ability to recruit new staff. It has been essential, for the purposes of staff cohesion, that staff be committed to changes proposed by Mandie – and by listening and acting upon their interests, she optimised her chances of success in the reconstruction of the curriculum.

In common with both Fulbridge and Dale, Mandie suggests that the success of her approach also depends heavily on teachers' own interests being placed more centre stage than a National Curriculum allows for, whilst bearing in mind that the demands of the curriculum are still present. This is not an easy circle to square and some staff felt the stresses only too keenly: 'I just wanted to put my head on the table and cry', said one teacher when faced with another of Mandie's rug-pulling moments.

In her criticism of the National Curriculum, the QCA and architects' school plans, Mandie also exemplifies the qualities needed to radically innovate and to move from a cautious, step-by-step incrementalism to a more full-blooded approach, not being afraid to challenge the status quo, feeling comfortable with high levels of risk and being able to see the challenges through, in both encouraging and disheartening times.

Is there anyone in your school who pulls the rug out from under your feet? Is this a creative decision or a disruptive one? Or a bit of both? At what points can creative teaching become disruptive learning? And how would you manage that tension? What would your success indicators be? How would you know and what evidence would you be able to use?

Notes

1   Visit http://www.qcda.gov.uk/default.aspx for further information about the QCA guidelines.
2   http://curriculum.qcda.gov.uk/key-stages-3-and-4/skills/plts/index.aspx.

References

Dewey, J. (1897) 'My pedagogic creed', *The School Journal*, 54(3): 77–80.
Sanders, E. (2010) *Leading a Creative School: Learning about Lasting School Change*, London: David Fulton.

Think, Connect, Act
Belfairs High School, Southend

Chris Reck

Editor's introduction

This chapter focuses on how children develop as independent thinkers and learners, and identifies a number of strategies which encourage young people to think about, and learn from, their own learning styles. It also demonstrates the importance of role modelling uncertainty in the thinking process. In addition to working with the Alite Learning to Learn (L2L) programme with its emphasis on

- resilience;
- resourcefulness;
- reasoning; and
- reflection and responsibility,

the school also focuses on and embeds a particular cluster of thinking skills across the school curriculum, including:

- locating information;
- organising and make sensing of information;
- judging information;
- transferring information; and
- innovation.

It also offers ideas for developing the self-motivation of students through a range of strategies which call for a slowing of the pace of thinking and learning.

The chapter presents a model of personalised, creative learning from the point of view of an English teacher, Chris Reck, who has taught English for many years in secondary education and who has in recent times found himself questioning and challenging many of the conditions that surround that practice, and increasingly criticising the climate in which those conditions flourish.

The voice in the wilderness: do you hear yourself in this picture?

Chris has not found the process of innovation easy, for either himself, the students he teaches or even his colleagues in the wider school community, and his frank and critical viewpoint opens up several immediate questions:

Is it possible to innovate the curriculum in isolated pockets of expertise in a school?

If so, what are the conditions that can help that individual to succeed?

Can there be islands of good practice?

Does every school need a lone voice in the curriculum wilderness to provide the impetus for more systemic change? Or are lone voices destined to stay unheard and unappreciated until they leave the building?

FIGURE 4.1 A typical climate in secondary schools?

The school context

Belfairs High School is a large comprehensive in Leigh-on-Sea in Essex which has developed an increasingly vocational curriculum in order to attract a wide range of pupils. In addition, it has also developed a curriculum which is based not just around subject knowledge but also on understanding what attributes enhance learning: how pupils learn to learn is seen as important as what they learn.

My focus in recent years has been the transition process from Key Stage 2 to Key Stage 3. My interest in English and concern for what my students are expected to cope with during their educational experience has led me to question many aspects of the system within which I work and to question how feasible it is to embed learning when colleagues and I are teaching perhaps up to 150 students a week who are receiving many different, disparate learning experiences.

The challenge for Chris and his colleagues

We need to be developing flexible thinking skills and connection-making skills. Students themselves, at first, are quite resistant towards this because they want knowledge to be delivered – spoon-fed – to them so that they can regurgitate it. Whilst there is recognition that connectivity and creativity are highly important aspects of thinking and

FIGURE 4.2 Leading the way to Belfairs High School

learning, as a teacher you have to demonstrate consistency in terms of trying to make these flexible thinking connections across the curriculum. You have to role model the thinking process and you have to role model its contingencies and its uncertainties and bring them into the classroom. It's very much like neurolinguistic practitioners, I believe, who say that the heart of everything comes from language. As an English teacher, I always remember a quote from Ezra Pound in which he talks about poetry and says that 'Great literature is simply language charged with meaning to the utmost possible degree', and I think the learning experience has to be language that is charged with thinking experience.

But you have to give students the language and you have to make that language live and breathe. One of the ways to do that is to go through the learning experience with them: scaffolding the learning by using open questions. If you were to come into my lessons, you would not only hear open questions, but you would also see me challenging the difficulties behind the learning process. Some students got upset with me about that because they just wanted the right answer and they wanted to know what they had to know in order to get through the exams. That wasn't good enough for me. This process is about developing flexible thinking skills that they can take out of school and use somewhere else.

Questions for consideration: Learning to Learn or learning to earn?

Chris suggests that there are two agendas at work in the school: the desire to develop an ever-increasing vocational curriculum, with its emphasis on real-world skills which prepare students for the world of work; and the desire to develop 'learning to learn' skills, or metacognition skills, which aim to develop students' critical thinking skills and 'learning muscles', to borrow a phrase from Guy Claxton. Is there a possibility that these two agendas are in competition? That a vocational agenda is not best served by processes which emphasise the intellectual nature of the learning process? And what about the role of subject knowledge in this mix of agendas? Is there now no room for subject knowledge at all?

Cast of characters/actors

Chris Reck   Advanced skills teacher, English
Clare St John Coleman   Advanced skills teacher, English

Timeline

September 2007   Learning to Learn programme begins
November 2008 to July 2009   Action research for Building Learning Power

The school started the 'Learning to Learn' programme in September 2007 with Year 7 pupils, which involved developing attributes for learning which, according to ALITE (Smith *et al.*, 2009), are constructed around the 5 Rs of:

FIGURE 4.3 The consequences of an ever-increasing vocational curriculum?

- Resilience (sticking at it, having a positive attitude, finding interest in what they are doing, setting targets and practising);
- Resourcefulness (using imagination, learning in different ways, asking good questions, taking risks);
- Reasoning (saying which is better and why, considering all the evidence, choosing the best method and working it through);
- Reflection (asking 'why?', staying calm, listening to different opinions and learning from mistakes);
- Responsibility (knowing right and wrong, getting on with it, taking time to help others).

In addition to the L2L programme, the school also wanted to focus on and embed a particular cluster of thinking skills across the school curriculum, listed below:

- how to locate information, recall, collate, sort;
- how to organise and make sense of information – classify, explain, relate, compare;
- how judge the worth of information – interrogate for bias, assign value, establish criteria, explore consequences;

- how to transfer information – reframe, hypothesise, focus on outcomes, construct arguments;
- how to innovate – ask questions, apply anew, adopt and adapt, imagine.

Questions for consideration

How would you assess this menu of thinking skills? What's missing? Do you detect a bias here? Are there certain students this menu would particularly suit? Whom would it not suit?

Motivating students in the classroom

I started by wanting to know the literature about how to motivate students in the classroom (Deci, 1996). I wanted to know if there was research that recognised absorption – 'lostness' – in learning, because of my own understanding of learning. I know that my own pleasure when learning is prompted by playfulness, serendipity, irreverence: what Carol Dweck (2007) refers to as a 'grace period'. I therefore had to develop and choreograph a portfolio of strategies in my teaching that allowed students to 'let go' whilst at the same time developing a sense of self-directed autonomy.

FIGURE 4.4 Lost in learning

I started to take risks in the classroom by stepping outside the parameters of the curriculum and its 'content-heaviness'. The strategies I was using called for slowing the pace of thinking and learning. I said to students, 'Right, we are going to start off with connection making and we're going to start off with the originality of your thought process.' This was great for me in English because I wanted to know how they felt about what a poet was trying to say. I didn't want the 'right answer', but I did want some interesting questions. So we looked at questions driving the learning process, and they found that quite uncomfortable at first. But I aimed to consistently use the same language with them, so they eventually became familiar with what I was asking for. The language I use is based around the questions:

- How do we learn today?
- What do we learn today?
- Why are we learning today?
- How do we go about learning today?
- What is difficult?
- How could we have done that differently?

Questions for consideration

Chris's idiosyncratic approach is particularly clear here. Would this be of any benefit in your classroom? How does this compare with your own approach? What kind of students would benefit from this type of approach? And which students are more likely to be turned off by it?

The risks in the process

Slowing down the class, however, does conflict with the tyranny of the timetable, which demands very little deviation from what is supposed to be achieved in a given week or half term. So for a teacher it is a risk.

It is risky in other respects too. I don't tell the students what they are learning: I negotiate with them. This requires a receptivity to their ideas that takes time and requires trust. Teachers find this difficult within the frenetic environment of a classroom dynamic. The students themselves are also used to a diet of measurable criteria. Some questioned the direction the learning was taking. Essentially, I had to role model the learning I was trying to nurture and this required optimism and persistence.

FIGURE 4.5 Risks in learning and assessment

Questions for consideration

Is this an approach you would feel comfortable to use in your classroom? If not, why not? Given the evident student resistance to this approach, can you imagine a conversation between students before and after they entered Chris's classroom? And what might that imagined conversation tell you?

How did he go about this?

I used music to accompany the different shades and moods of learning; started reading stories that made connections with the dispositions that signified their development as successful learners; and devised play breaks to re-energise and focus both myself and the students during learning.

I created visual images to reflect upon and chart the 'thinking' and 'feelings' that underpin learning; I started to apologise when I got things wrong or created misunderstandings, because I realised that I had to role model that successful learners admit when they make mistakes, that success is about reframing failure.

FIGURE 4.6 Providing challenging questions

I focused on good questions (Koechlin and Zwann, 2006), not correct answers; reflected upon the necessary and healthy struggle that is what I call 'the DNA of learning'. I wanted to use language in a contagious way so as to construct and connect thinking and learning.

I monitored this process through filming it and sharing it with the students, and through questionnaires derived from Claxton's Building Learning Power. The school also set up a mentoring system based on the identified attributes and thinking skills of Learning to Learn, which were monitored through Learning to Learn department meetings and anecdotal feedback. Two external assessments were also delivered by the school.

I used some of the questionnaires provided by the Learning to Learn programme, but these were soon superseded by a number of methods which I used to stimulate this work. I call them strategies, but they might just as usefully be seen as the tactic of using 'open questions' to elicit analogous thinking and cognitive awareness.

Relating understanding of one domain of thinking to another is a highly creative process and introduces students to the concept of relatedness, with the ultimate aim of breaking down the barriers of compartmentalised learning. The more connections you make, the more autonomous you are in your choices of connection making. The point for the teacher is to let the students eventually take over the process.

The following section provides a selection of strategies that I used during this period. They are not intended to be sequential, progressive or used in any particular structural manner, but they have provided me with the means to engage students and challenge them to consider how they learn and what learning is all about.

Covey's work on promoting 'habits' of connecting learning

I used this model to promote 'habits' of connecting learning and to construct learning intentions and journeys (Covey, 2004). These tactics were employed in every lesson. It wasn't easy though, and I had to persist and hard-wire it into the students' learning repertoire. This involved constantly referring to a number of guiding questions:

- 'What are we learning?' because it raises awareness;
- 'Why are we learning this?' because it raises debates about relevance and motivation; and
- 'How will we learn?' because it helps students to reflect upon the skills required to make progress.

The great thing about choreographing learning in this way is that it promotes reflection and develops a habit of thinking for both students and teacher whereby process overrides content – although this could well be a high-risk strategy for pupils and teachers for whom content and subject matter are of some significance.

Questions for consideration

Chris's notion that learning is choreographed is a useful metaphor in that it suggests the possibility of all kinds of movement by its participants. What kind of movement would the techniques he describes generate in your classroom? Creative, free-flowing, contemporary contact improvisation? The military two-step? Anarchy? Are there elements of Chris's approach which you could adapt for your own 'choreographed learning' spaces, i.e. classrooms?

A menu that brought these approaches together is what I call the 'Reflection menu', taken and customised from Barry Hymer's *Gifted and Talented Pocketbook*. My 'Reflection menu' is as follows:

Reflection menu
Please share your course with the whole class . . .

Reflection starter
What do you want to learn today?
What skills do you have that could be useful this lesson?
What might hinder your thinking?

When have you had to think like this before?
What have you learned that is similar?
What do you already know that might be useful?
What must you do in this lesson? What should you do? What could you do?

Reflection main courses
What are you currently thinking about?
Has any of the lesson so far been about you?
What connections have you made?
How do you feel about the lesson?
How have you got involved in the lesson?
What should you do to further your thinking?
What breakthroughs have you made?
What do you want to know more about?

Reflection desserts
How are you going to remember this learning?
What is the key aspect you will remember from this lesson?
What has this lesson reminded you of?
Which senses were most important?
What did you learn that you didn't know before?
What have you learned that could be useful elsewhere?
What have you learned elsewhere that is like this?
How will you apply what you have learned?

(At certain points in the lesson students will be invited to think-pair-share their choice of course.)

If you have any suggestions as to how we can improve your thinking and learning experiences please do not hesitate to inform us. Kind regards: Learning Management.

Questions for consideration

How would your students respond to these kinds of questions? Are there limits to the effectiveness of this kind of reflection in your classroom? What might you need in your classroom to undertake this process? When might this process not be of use?

The influence of the neuroscience of learning

Another area of research which I was interested in was that of the neuroscience of learning (Feinstein, 2004). Teachers need to know what's 'beneath the bonnet' and they need to be conversant with some basic neuroscience of how a teenager's brain works. There are a number of aspects of this research which I have used to understand how teenagers learn:

FIGURE 4.7 The neuroscience of learning?

- 'play breaks' promote balance, well-being and laughter, as described in Looms and Kolberg's *The Laughing Classroom*;
- 'mirror neurons' in the cortex are developing during teenage years and predispose young people to mimic what they see others doing;
- the reticular activating system, the 'central commanding system of the brain', causes us to focus our attention on learning.

Questions for consideration

Do you think this kind of 'scientific' thinking has a role in the understanding of learning in the classroom? What are its benefits? What are the implications of connecting recent thinking in neurological science with the day-to-day realities of teaching in the classroom? Is 'getting under the bonnet' of a teenager's brain a useful metaphor for how a young person's mind might work and how a young person might learn?

This research is combined with a series of strategies which can be categorised under three headings:

- connection making;
- review and reflection;
- dissemination.

Connection-making strategies

- *Connections board*. Designate display space for interesting connections between subjects that can be displayed using Post-It notes.

- *Connections diary*. Have your own 'connections diary' so that you can write down connections (outrageous, profound or otherwise) that your students share with you.

- *Connections treasure chest*. Place Post-It note connections in a 'treasure chest' (can be made from a shoebox) so that you can treasure the thoughts of your students and come back to them in future weeks, months, years.

- *Random words*. This is based on De Bono's tables of random words exercises (De Bono, 2008). You have to create six tables of words that comprise six columns and six rows of six words, so that each of the six tables is made up of 216 words. You then need to download a dice from the internet and cut and paste it on to a PowerPoint slide. Distribute the tables of random words to the students and devise games that require making connections between the randomly selected words, using the dice. The range of possibilities is endless: e.g. select four words (potato, carousel, holiday, metal detector) and explain which is the odd word out by conceptually connecting the other three words. Use the table of random words to make connections between subjects, to write poems, stories, make connections with characters from history, etc. You don't have to rely on a downloaded dice, of course; you can give individuals, pairs or groups of students a dice so that they can play on their own.

- *Question builder frames*. I have found these particularly successful for reticent students, but they work for all so-called ability levels (one probably should say 'confidence' levels). Take 'who, what, when, where, why, how, which' and attach the words 'are, was, were, did, does, can, could, would, should, will, might'. Experiment with these prompts using surrealist paintings so that students feel comfortable with asking probing and searching questions: for example, encourage 'what might' rather than 'what is' questions so as to nurture more searching questions. Turn it into a game where you choose the question prompt.

- *Motivational statements*. You don't need to spend the school budget on buying a book of motivational statements and having them photocopied and laminated and placed around the school. It is much easier to visit of several hundred websites and cut and paste statements to a PowerPoint slideshow. Use custom animation so that each quote is slowly revealed – try it as a rogue slide in the middle of a lesson. Take a break and discuss its significance. Can we connect it to our current learning?

- *Connection-making bridges*. This involves designing a bridge, either in the form of a classroom poster, an actual bridge, or a PowerPoint slide that invites students to connect their learning from a previous lesson with the learning that is about to take place in yours. This requires role modelling from the teacher in the form of:

> Where were you last lesson? Geography? What did you learn? You learned about the stages that lead to volcanoes erupting? OK, so how can I connect that with our learning today, which is about Victor Frankenstein and his desire to create everlasting life? Perhaps I can interpret Victor's ambition as causing an eruption,

a lava flow of unforeseen consequences. Thank you, you have now given me a powerful image that allows me to explore Victor's motivation in a more creative and expressive way.

Questions for consideration

Chris places a great store in the need to *connect*. But what might be the limits to this approach? How does making connection embed into deeper and more consistent on-going learning? Will it help the anxious student to pass their GCSEs? And does it matter if it doesn't?

Review and reflection strategies

- *Feelings thermometer*. This thermometer is based on Mihaly Csikszentmihalyi's (2007) theory of the processes that underpin acquiring skills sets: if your lessons require low skills sets, then you will induce apathy and boredom; however, if you are going to acquire challenging skills sets, then you have to be prepared to struggle before reaching a point where you have acquired mastery and control. This thermometer focuses on those feelings: boredom/apathy, worry/concern, struggle/challenging, feeling in control, wanting to know more, 'flow' feelings. Use it to measure your students' feelings during the course of your lesson. Staff observe students overcoming struggle and gaining confidence and then reference it to the 'feelings thermometer'. The feelings thermometer is always visible in the classroom as a reference point for the feelings we experience when learning. The teacher incorporates this language into supporting and guiding student motivation.

- *Thinking thermometer*, based on Bloom's Revised Taxonomy (Anderson *et al.*, 2001). Develop a chart that measures the level of thinking that has been generated in the lesson: e.g. have we been remembering, understanding, applying, analysing, evaluating, creating? Where would you place your thinking today on the thinking chart? What level of thinking do I need to plan into the next lesson? Put your suggestions on a Post-It note so that I can get an idea of where you think you are on the thinking thermometer. This thermometer is a reference point. It also challenges the teacher to think about whether low-level, medium-level or higher-level thinking skills have been used in the lesson. It is a visual reference that is in the classroom.

- *The iceberg*. Use the image of an iceberg to promote 'deeper' thinking according to the assessment criteria of your subject area. Renegotiate the language of assessment with your students to encourage them to explore what lies 'beneath the surface'. Place that language on the iceberg.

- *Change the language of assessment*. Ask students to come up with different language. For example, one of my students told me she was bored with being 'evaluated'. So we had a discussion based around how you 'grow' as a learner. This led to 'greenhouse' and 'composting' stages of learning.

■ *Learner journals/diaries.* Order A4 exercise books that have blank rather than lined pages so that students can doodle and draw whilst thinking. Encourage them to use different colours whilst taking notes. This breaks down inhibitions about 'being' or 'not being' perfect. If they want to write on lines, then they can use a ruler in their books. Encourage creativity, don't suppress it. Assignments/homework can be presented neatly after due reflection.

Questions for consideration

The importance of reflection is another important aspect to Chris's approach to pedagogy. But, as in the case of connection making, there are also limits to the value of reflecting. What might they be? And again, how does an approach which favours deep reflection embed into more consistent ongoing learning? And in the case of the anxious, grade-fixated student and their parent – could you argue the value of this pedagogy on a cold, wet parents' evening in November?

Dissemination strategies

■ *Film your lessons.* This gives the opportunity to play back students' learning to them so that they can reflect upon it. This is combined with a template of questions that are based on developing their learning dispositions:

- What did you think of today's lesson?

- What went well?

- What didn't go well?

- What did you find difficult?

- How did you overcome that difficulty?

- What was easy? If it was too easy how could you make it more difficult? Did you learn from anybody else other than the teacher?

- How could the teacher improve the lesson next time? What advice would you give the teacher to improve?

■ *Flip-chart paper displays.* Record learning on to flip-chart paper and put it up on the wall at the moment of learning. Learning is not neat and tidy; it is often messy and disjointed. Your classroom displays should reflect this. Neatness often engenders anxiety.

■ *Personal responsibility lessons.* Take time out of the curriculum to teach two lessons that can be found in 'Learning to listen and sabotage' in Paul Ginnis's *The Teacher's Toolkit*. Then get volunteer teachers from your class to teach one year group below. Allow the teacher-students to come to school that day dressed in smart, business-like dress and allow them time to prepare the lesson with the teacher. Film the preparation and delivery of the lesson. Play the film back to the teacher-students and reflect upon the 'thinking' and 'feelings' process of their experience. Extend the process further by contacting a 'feeder' school so that Year 7 can then go and teach Year 5 what they learned from Year 9 about 'learning to listen'. It takes some organising, but you are sowing the seeds of what a real 'learning community' should be.

Questions for consideration

Dissemination, reflection and connection making constitute the main thrust of Chris's pedagogical approach. What are the limits to this pedagogy? What are its strengths? Is this an approach which you can see would transform learning in your school?

I noted that at first there was reluctance from the students to see the validity in these approaches, which could be due to their being conditioned to look for certainties rather than possibilities in their thinking and learning. But after persistence on the part of both the students and myself, I found that these strategies opened up whole new avenues for students to personally connect with learning. After you have role modelled the process of connection making you will find that students automatically start to make connections for themselves and volunteer to walk across the connection-making bridge that exists both between subject areas and in life.

Well, so what?

These strategies may all be very well – but in the end, if this approach to innovation is going to have some effect, teachers will want to know what happened as a result of these approaches – and whether any long-standing change was brought about in students' learning. Can you see how you could use the strategies listed above in your school?

Can you identify how they might be used progressively, rather than as an ad hoc series of tactics? How might you evaluate the impact of these strategies on students' attainment and attitude to learning?

Chris was only too well aware of the need to monitor and evaluate. As ever with the case of trying to justify the effects of a particular intervention or initiative, it is difficult to extract the rhetoric which presents itself as leading to the best possible impact, from the data which one can feel confidence in. Chris suggests that his approach contributed to a significant increase in the results being achieved at KS3 and KS4, after the local context is taken into account, although quite what the direct relationship was between his work and those indicators is very difficult to say.

How would you evaluate his success? How would you communicate that success? Would you expect to see a change in attainment? Pupil engagement? Attendance? Morale?

Evaluation: measuring the immeasurable?

At the start of the year I used questionnaires that focused on attitudes to learning – in particular, attitudes towards getting stuck, making mistakes, planning, collaboration. I measured those attitudes every half term so that students could reflect on the progress they had made in terms of their attributes. During the year I encouraged staff to observe my lessons, collected portfolios of students' work (mainly video evidence) and held half termly meetings with Learning to Learn teachers where they reflected not only on students' development but also on their own as teachers.

The Learning to Learn teaching group was comprised of volunteers made up of subject leaders, senior managers, one deputy head and two advanced skills teachers (including myself): all experienced teachers receptive to developing their teaching practice. At the end of the year the questionnaires were revisited, students were filmed and interviewed and an external agency was brought in to evaluate and offer suggestions for improvement and development. A recent Ofsted report referred to lessons that encouraged students to think things out for themselves: attributes that epitomise the aim of learning to learn and the connection-making process.

Questions for consideration

Are there other types of evaluation that would be more useful in assessing the effectiveness of this approach? Is there a danger that using old tools to measure new methods only shows up the limits of the tools and hides the value of the methods?

The end-game. . .

I eventually became disillusioned with the school's unwillingness to commit towards extending the L2L capacity. Senior management viewed the teachers who delivered it as 'special' teachers who had the skills set to develop it discretely, and this contributed to the sense that this innovation was somehow too 'out-there', one step too far to take, to warrant any further substantial organisational investment. I took a certain amount of comfort from regarding myself as one minute an *agent provocateur* and the next hugely humbled by the gifts that L2L allowed students to unearth about themselves. There was management support in the sense that there was a raised awareness of the need for L2L. But there was never really an understanding of how it could be embedded across the school. We had only got to phase one.

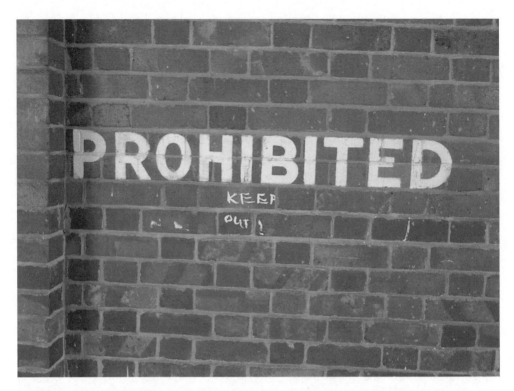

FIGURE 4.8 The End Game?

Matters for consideration: embedding the work across the school

Chris acknowledges that a great deal of energy was spent in winning colleagues around, and in a difficult climate. An external assessment reference to the L2L programme demonstrated that it needed to be embedded across the school and part of the whole school culture, with just the right mix of coercion with nurture. It couldn't function as a discrete, once-a-week lesson that was then not reinforced in other lessons. What structures or processes are available in your school to ensure that innovation initiatives can be disseminated across the staff group? Innovation is sometimes seen as requiring the work of an independent voice, a maverick or someone who stands outside the normal school operating environment. Do you recognise that archetype in your school? How does your school deal with or contain that difference?

References

Anderson, L.W., Krathwohl, D.R., Airasian, P.W., Cruikshank, K.A., Mayer, R.E., Pintrich, P.R., Raths, J. and Wittrock, M.C. (eds) (2001) *A Taxonomy for Learning, Teaching, and Assessing – A Revision of Bloom's Taxonomy of Educational Objectives*, Addison Wesley Longman, Inc.

Covey, S. (2004) *The Seven Habits of Highly Effective People*, Simon and Schuster Ltd.

Csikszentmihalyi, M. (1997) *Finding Flow: The Psychology of Engagement with Everyday Life*, New York: Basic Books.

De Bono, E. (2008) *How To Have Creative Ideas. 62 Exercises To Develop the Mind*, Vermilion.

Deci, E.L. (1996) *Why We Do What We Do: Understanding Self-Motivation*, Harmondsworth: Penguin Books.

Dweck, C.S. (2007) *Mindset: The New Psychology of Success*, Random House Publishing Group.

Feinstein, S. (2004) *Secrets of the Teenage Brain – Research-Based Strategies for Reaching and Teaching Today's Adolescents*, Corin Press.

Ginnis, P. (2001) *Teacher's Toolkit: Raise Classroom Achievement with Strategies for Every Learner*, Crown House Publishing.

Hymer, B. (2009) *Gifted and Talented Pocketbook*, Management Pocketbooks.

Koechlin, C. and Zwann, S. (2006) *Q Tasks: How To Empower Students To Ask Questions and Care about Answers*, Pembroke Publishers Ltd.

Looms, D. and Kolberg, K. (2003) *The Laughing Classroom: Everyone's Guide to Teaching with Humor and Play*, H J Kramer.

Smith, A., Lovatt, M. and Turner, J. (2009) *Learning to Learn in Practice: The L2 Approach*, Crown House Publishing.

5

Leading from the Head, the Heart and the Whole Body

Kingstone School, Barnsley

Alistair Chambers

Editor's introduction

This chapter shows how a thematic approach to teaching collaboratively for cross-curriculum projects can be developed in a way that bridges the pedagogical gap which exists between high schools and their feeder primary schools. It highlights the use of established drama-based teaching conventions, such as Dorothy Heathcote's Mantle of the Expert in the humanities, in order to strengthen and deepen students' understanding. The chapter also shows how the personalisation agenda is reflected through project-based learning (PBL) in which teachers become able to develop alternative pedagogical strategies and teaching stances (Craft *et al.*, 2007).

Kingstone School in Barnsley has been involved with Creative Partnerships (CP) since 2003, when the current head teacher, Matthew Milburn, joined the school. At the time, he felt that the school's engagement with the creativity agenda wasn't particularly sustainable or transformational but, following discussions with the regional director for CP, Dave Gilbert, he developed some ideas about how they might work together to change the curriculum with the support of CP.

Matthew identified a group of teachers who were interested in changing the way in which they taught, particularly in Key Stage 3. It happened that they all came from the humanities area and this allowed them to talk about creating a more thematic approach which had drama at its centre, as opposed to the discrete subjects themselves.

This initial impetus from the head was developed over the following six years and, in contrast to the Belfairs story, is a critical example of how leadership needs to be distributed through the whole school community if innovation is to take root and flourish: from its head, to a heart of committed and interested teachers, and then across the whole body of staff and students.

Introduction: the school context

Teachers at Kingstone had observed that pupils left their primary schools full of enthusiasm for learning but rapidly lost their eagerness between the ages of 11 and 14. The successes that our feeder schools were enjoying led us to consider the pedagogical differences between primary and secondary teaching. Like most high schools, we traditionally favoured pigeon-holing subjects taught by different teachers, whereas primary schools prefer a single teacher to deliver topics, which allows for the detailed exploration of the various strands of the National Curriculum. We expect our pupils to move from classroom to classroom, learning in hourly sessions that have finite beginnings and endings. Our pupils have insufficient time to explore their own questions because of demands on teachers for pace and progression.

FIGURE 5.1
Sustaining the enthusiasm for learning

The Year 6–Year 7 transition debate

Alistair suggests that the pedagogical approaches of primary school should be mirrored more closely in secondary schools, particularly in Year 7, to help the transition between the two phases. Do you agree that there is such a gulf between primary and secondary schools? Is it an inevitable consequence of the way schools are structured? Many secondary schools have developed bridging or transition projects which aim to bridge this gulf, for example, by sending secondary school teachers into the partner primary schools. With what initiatives has your school been involved in helping to bridge this gap between primary and secondary phases?

Matthew Milburn, head teacher at Kingstone, invited teachers who were interested in adopting a thematic approach to teaching to collaborate in order to develop a curriculum that could be delivered to our Year 7s. We wanted this curriculum to bridge the gulf in pedagogy that exists between high schools and their feeders. Those who volunteered consisted for the most part of teachers of the humanities, as well as teachers of drama.

We decided to combine subjects in the thematic programme known as Cultural Studies (CS) – geography, history, RE, PHSCE, citizenship and drama, with ICT being incorporated at a later stage.

Questions for discussion

The model for curriculum change here is based on the notion that change can be initiated by a small group of teachers – the vanguard – who can lead to bigger, whole school change; as opposed to a structural approach, which argues that school change comes about by changing school organisational structures and processes. Is that a model which would work in your school? What are its limitations? And what are its advantages?

Cast of characters/actors

Matthew Milburn	Head teacher, Kingstone School
Ondrie Mann	Geography teacher
Debbie Kidd	Creative friend
Charlie Brammer	Assistant head in charge of specialism (Performing Arts)
Jane Hewitt	Advanced skills teacher
Dorothy Heathcote	Mantle of the Expert

Timeline

February 2003	Started working with Creative Partnerships
Spring 2004	Members of staff interested in pedagogical reform identified. Coordinator of project appointed.
Summer 2004	INSET led by Debbie Kidd to prepare team for Cultural Studies pilot.
September 2005	Four Year 7 forms began Cultural Studies, whilst the remaining six forms continued to be taught discrete Geography, History, RE, PHSCE, Citizenship and Drama lessons.
September 2006	Cultural Studies rolled out to entire year group.
September 2007	Curriculum for Confidence introduced as a means of tapering thematic learning into discrete subject delivery.
July 2008	Assessment for Living piloted with two Year 7 forms as an innovative way of assessing holistic learning.
July 2009	Assessment for Living rolled out to entire year group and piloted in Year 8 with original two forms.
July 2010	Assessment for Living rolled out to all of Year 8 in addition to Year 7.

List of activities

Plots and Protests: comparing peaceful protest (Civil Rights Movement) to violent protest (Gunpowder Plot)

Child Labour

The Boy in the Striped Pyjamas

FIGURE 5.2 Students debating *The Boy in the Striped Pyjamas*

FIGURE 5.3 Role play in the Mantle of the Expert

British Culture and Identity
Mantle of the Expert project (various)
Assessment for Living

Adopting the mantles of the experts

As a school with Performing Arts status, an emerging priority was also the use of drama across the curriculum. Matthew's background as a drama teacher and his involvement in the National Association for the Teaching of Drama meant that he saw the potential of introducing established drama-based teaching conventions into the humanities in order to strengthen and deepen students' understanding.

The work of Dorothy Heathcote and her 'Mantle of the Expert' programme offered especial potential. One of the main aims of the introduction of Mantle of the Expert, amongst other tools, was to help pupils to empathise with people from different places and points in time to their own – with obvious implications for geography and history.

FIGURE 5.4 Mantle of the Expert: helping pupils to empathise with people from different places and other points in time

What is the Mantle of the Expert?[1]

The Mantle of the Expert is a dramatic inquiry-based approach to teaching and learning invented and developed by Professor Dorothy Heathcote at the University of Newcastle upon Tyne in the 1980s. The big idea is that the class do all their curriculum work as if they are an imagined group of experts. They might be scientists in a laboratory, archaeologists excavating a tomb or a rescue team at the scene of a disaster. They might be running a removal company, a factory, a shop, a space station or a French resistance group. Because they behave 'as if they are experts', the children are working from a specific point of view as they explore their learning, and this brings special responsibilities, language needs and social behaviours. Let us be clear: the children are not putting on a play or running a business. They are simply being asked to agree, for a time, to imagine themselves as a group of scientists, archaeologists or librarians with jobs and responsibilities. Through activities and tasks, the children gradually take on the same kinds of responsibilities, problems and challenges that real archaeologists, scientists and librarians might do in the real world.

The gathering of the clans

Having identified those members of staff who were keen to embrace this style of teaching, Matthew appointed Ondrie Mann, a geography teacher, to lead the process of change. Matthew also asked Debbie Kidd, 'Creative friend', to assist in the formation of the programme. Kingstone was allotted roughly 60 school days-worth of Debbie's time, to be funded by Creative Partnerships. Debbie was given the title of 'Creative friend' whilst at Kingstone, and her role was primarily to work with Ondrie in order to provide him with the skills to use drama in Cultural Studies. In addition, Debbie was asked to liaise with those colleagues involved in the project to help them develop the programme in a self-sustaining way. Opportunities were provided for members of staff who had not opted into Cultural Studies to observe these lessons in order to give them an insight into this approach to teaching and learning.

Points of drama

Ten days of INSET were set aside. We worked with the children from four out of the ten forms, and in the second year we rolled it out to all of Year 7; in the third year we then incorporated a Year 8 course, called Curriculum for Confidence based on the fact that the children had low self-esteem.

However, there was a perception amongst some members of staff that this planning was being done behind closed doors, and this generated a substantial feeling of suspicion towards Cultural Studies in the staffroom. None of the group who were involved in the process of change anticipated the level of negativity they encountered as a result of their participation in Cultural Studies.

FIGURE 5.5 Collaborating on the floor in Cultural Studies

Teachers were clustered in teams of three or four to work with a single form group, the intention being that each class would have access to Drama, Geography, History and RE specialists (although this did not always prove to be feasible). Most of the teachers were in more than one team and were timetabled to deliver between one and seven hours per class per fortnight. Attempts were made to cluster experienced teachers with those relatively new to the profession, and teachers whose classrooms were located close to one another. It was suggested that each group should be given a 'base' in the form of one classroom where their work could always be displayed.

The power of drama in placing students at the heart of creative learning

Kingstone used the work of Dorothy Heathcote and the Mantle of the Expert approach as a key resource in changing its curriculum for Year 7 pupils.

According to the website,[2] in the Mantle of the Expert there is always an 'enterprise' to be run, and always a client who needs help with a job needing to be done. The emphasis is on the tasks the children need to do so as to make the 'enterprise' a success and to serve the needs of the clients. The system permits the normal school context of class responsibility to change. Instead of the children relying on the teacher's energy to drive the work and evaluate achievement, teacher and class share the responsibility for the quality of work. Running the enterprise is, like an enterprise in real-life, based in action and processes; thus it generates a range of different tasks: talking, listening, writing, speaking, making, designing, planning, measuring, weighing etc. These tasks are channelled by the teacher towards the requirements of the school curriculum.

Can you see potential 'enterprises' in your school which might benefit from such an approach? Mantle of the Expert also requires different teaching stances to be taken: can you identify what these might be and what this would mean for how a teacher might change their teaching styles in the classroom? Are there certain curriculum areas which would fit well with this approach? Or other areas which would not easily fit?

(Not) involving students

During our preparation for the pilot of Cultural Studies we did not make as much use of our pupils' views and opinions as we could have done, in order to stay true to the spirit of project-based learning. It was not a strategic decision that pupil voice would be overlooked, but rather it was a result of the initial difficulties we had in devising a curriculum that we agreed we could deliver and that fairly represented the range of subjects co-opted into Cultural Studies.

What is project-based learning?[3]

Project-based learning is a comprehensive instructional approach to engage students in sustained, cooperative investigation (Bransford and Stein, 1993). Within its framework, students collaborate, working together to make sense of what is going on. Project-based instruction differs from inquiry-based activity – activity most of us have experienced during our own schooling – in its emphasis on cooperative learning. Inquiry is traditionally thought of as an individually done, somewhat isolated activity.

Additionally, project-based instruction differs from traditional inquiry in its emphasis on students' own artefact construction to represent what is being learned. Students pursue solutions to nontrivial problems by asking and refining questions, debating ideas, making predictions, designing plans and/or experiments, collecting and analysing data, drawing conclusions, communicating their ideas and findings to others, asking new questions and creating artefacts (Blumenfeld et al., 1991).

Structures and processes

In order to allow for pupil co-construction in teaching and learning within the Cultural Studies pilot, we opted to use what became known as 'learning pathways' instead of traditional schemes of work (SoW). These differ from SoW in that they focus on existential and philosophical questions which we expect learners to develop answers to as they explore a topic.

Within the pathway documents there are suggestions about possible learning opportunities, but the way in which these are exploited is left to the discretion of the teacher and class. Use of these was inconsistent during the pilot because some teachers embraced the uncertainty of allowing their pupils to take decisions about the direction their learning was to take, whilst others resorted to making choices on behalf of their students about what to learn.

Questions for consideration

'Co-construction' of learning is a much-vaunted concept in personalised learning agendas[4] and is implicit in project-based learning approaches. But what does it mean to you in practice? Do you know of valuable examples of co-constructed learning? Or other examples which 'talk the talk' but fail to 'construct the construct'? What might be useful criteria for a co-constructed learning approach?

Evaluating progress

In order to evaluate the effectiveness of the programme, pupils were selected at random from the Cultural Studies pilot to give their perspectives on the teaching and learning taking place in their lessons.

FIGURE 5.6 Co-construction company at work

The responses they gave helped to inform the changes which were made to the course between its initial trial and its blanket introduction to Year 7 in 2006. We considered pupils' opinions when evaluating the content covered during the pilot, as well as the effectiveness of the new pedagogy. As such, it is the refinement process that has benefited most from the pupil voice, and continued dialogue between staff and pupils means that Cultural Studies remains a very dynamic programme in its sixth year.

Pupils told us that Cultural Studies worked best when staff collaborated effectively with one another. In its infancy, teachers of the same class attempted to 'pass the baton' of learning to one another through discussion, e-mail, etc. Despite our best efforts this often proved very difficult, and again a lack of consistency between teachers emerged. Some took great care to ensure that the colleague following them was fully informed about a class's progress, but others found it more difficult to guarantee this. The pupils told us that a common reason that they did not enjoy Cultural Studies lessons was that their teachers repeated the same lesson when they had failed to liaise with others in their team. Through these interviews it also became increasingly clear that students received widely varying experiences of Cultural Studies, depending on their teachers. Following feedback from the pilot, Kingstone's Senior Leadership Team attempted to allocate one teacher to deliver all of a given form's Cultural Studies lessons. The response from pupils was that Cultural Studies lessons were much more enjoyable and meaningful when taught in this way.

FIGURE 5.7 Student voice in Cultural Studies

Those teachers currently delivering Cultural Studies have, for the most part, been involved in the project since its pilot year. As our understanding of the pedagogy behind the programme has developed, our confidence in giving students more control over the direction of their learning has increased. This is because teachers understand more fully why it is incumbent on them to relinquish their traditional role as givers of knowledge. Our own learning journey has reinforced that pupils will learn most effectively when they are given the chance to answer the questions that occur to them rather than the ones that we think they should be examining.

Becoming an expert at being an expert

Listening to and acting upon student voice[5] is clearly integral to the success of an approach which relies on Mantle of the Expert as it main pedagogical driver. It is clear though, from Alistair's account, that engaging student voice was not as straightforward a process as might have at first appeared. What policies and procedures do you have in place to promote student voice in your school? What have you learned from those experiences?

What happened next . . .?

Teachers who chose to become part of the Cultural Studies team have learned to be more creative and reflective. Speaking from the perspective of a Geography teacher who had not studied Drama since Year 9 and who had not relished the subject up to that point, I was surprised at how quickly I found myself immersed in the use of drama in the classroom. I then saw it as entirely appropriate that I apply the new skills that I acquired to my teaching across KS3, and even into KS4 at times, as did many other Cultural Studies teachers. Furthermore, members of the Cultural Studies team have gone on to lead INSET at school, local education authority and national events, in order to share their learning.

Matthew has fostered a culture at Kingstone that educators take creative risks in their work. He has constantly reassured us that we should not avoid risk-taking for fear of setbacks. It is now quite common for a classroom to contain groups of pupils around islands of desks, talking excitedly and noisily, scribbling notes on sugar paper, where only a few years ago they were expected to sit quietly in rows and the emphasis was on neatness and uniformity. Pupils are now just as likely to be found around school with video cameras as writing at desks or using computers.

The absence of silence in the classroom is not something that unduly worries Matthew. On the contrary, he sees silence as something which indicates oppression and compliance rather than as a sign of focused, concentrated learning. In referring to previous schools he had worked in, he points out:

> The problem at times was that it seemed more important to have a quiet and orderly classroom than a classroom where learning was taking place. In fact the two were confused: a quiet, orderly classroom means an orderly classroom. But it doesn't. It's perfectly possible to have complete silence in a room and no learning going on whatsoever.

The relationship between teacher and pupils has shifted substantially in many cases, with learners now being encouraged to question the ideas they are presented with and

FIGURE 5.8 The absence of silence in the classroom

to formulate their own opinions. Teachers have become highly reflexive, responding to students' queries with subtle questioning that helps young people to tap into their intrinsic understanding of the world in order to reach independent conclusions.

Just as Matthew emphasised the need for creative risk-taking by members of staff, Cultural Studies teachers have sought to show pupils that making mistakes, recognising them and rectifying them is an integral part of the learning process. Ample time is therefore given to reviewing and redrafting important pieces of work, with pupils being encouraged to evaluate their own work as well as that of their peers.

Risky noise or risk-free silence?

As in other case studies in this book, leaders across the school point to the need to encourage a risk-tolerant approach when it comes to moving towards a child-centred pedagogy of creative learning. In this instance, the presence of noise in a classroom means the presence of an interested and creative group of young people who are engaging with their learning in meaningful ways. Elsewhere, noise might indicate anarchy, lack of control and the absence of meaningful learning. What might be the characteristics of constructive noise and destructive noise in your classrooms?

Breadth at the expense of depth?

Concerns were raised that Cultural Studies failed to meet certain strands of its component subjects' programmes of study. Our learning pathways try to allow young people to discover things about the world that they can apply in many different settings. What starts as apparently narrow learning is therefore projected onto larger and larger scales so that pupils recognise links to situations from the past and from other places. Pupils are encouraged to take a holistic approach to their education so that they understand the links that exist in the knowledge that they have acquired at school and beyond it.

What's been learned: empathy

The Kingstone experience of project-based learning has shown that dramatic conventions can be used to create empathy in young people that exceeds anything previously seen in our school. This understanding of people in other situations often manifests itself at the most surprising of times. Matthew remembers when we had a remembrance service:

> and it was just so powerful and the children wanted to be quiet because they understood the implications of people fighting in order to gain freedom. Whether you agree or disagree with war, the fact is, men will have lost their lives to enable people to enjoy the freedoms that we enjoy. We had loads of veterans coming up to us afterwards to say that the children had been very good – and they were, because they understood why it was important for them to be so.

FIGURE 5.9 Breadth at the expense of depth?

FIGURE 5.10 Dramatic conventions are powerful in creating empathy in young people

Documenting progress

It also becomes clear when pupils are asked to ad-lib roles that these learning activities raise issues about documenting such learning. Archiving the work of pupils in Cultural Studies has necessitated the purchase of numerous digital media devices that allow young people and teachers to photograph, film, and record audio. We have learned that a reliable ICT infrastructure and good access to computers are essential in order to capitalise on opportunities for students to review their work digitally.

Cultural Studies has also shown that when pupils attain the status of active participants in lessons, and when the purpose and context of their work is clearly defined, they are able to write with a style and maturity that would not normally be expected in the humanities from Year 7s. Understanding of audience and purpose, whether they be real or fictional, seems to help young people construct arguments far more effectively than when they are asked to write in the abstract.

Questions for discussion

Alastair makes several claims about the effect of the Cultural Studies programme on the Year 7 students. What evidence would you look for to support these claims?

Common mistakes

Everyone who has taught Cultural Studies has made the mistake of setting tasks in a vague manner, using poorly thought-out instructions such as 'Imagine that you are Guy Fawkes and his co-conspirators. Create a piece of drama to show. . .' Such lack of clarity on the teacher's part has almost always resulted in students failing to meet learning objectives, and often ends in students' inability to manage themselves effectively.

Teachers have therefore recognised that it is incumbent on us to 'protect' students into their tasks by making sure that they understand and stay within important parameters – for example, their characters' backgrounds, their hopes, fears and so on. Matthew demonstrates how using the painting of the Guy Fawkes plotters within a dramatic framework can become a real, purposeful challenge for pupils:

> You recreate a still image of that and then you lock the door behind them and there is no way out for them, and suddenly you have got children who are going to have to hide inside the basement of the Houses of Parliament and make decisions about whose bloody idea was this in the first place.

Questions for consideration

If you were teaching this module on Guy Fawkes, how would you strengthen the exercise for pupils in order to ensure that they met their learning objectives? As well as asking students to imagine themselves in character, what additional information would they need? And at what point in the exercise?

What's been learned: new approaches to planning

Planning has taken a distinctly different turn with the adoption of the Mantle of the Expert approach. As Matthew has pointed out:

> I've never seen Dorothy write objectives on the board. I'd say she was an outstanding teacher but in Ofsted terms she can't be called outstanding because she hasn't written her objectives on the board. It's an absolute nonsense that there is one way to do it. I want there to be effective lessons, but that doesn't mean to say that the only way to have effective lessons is to describe the objectives at the beginning. The whole point of a dramatic reveal is that half way through the lesson the kids suddenly realise "oh my goodness – look at that!"

Questions for consideration

Matthew shows great faith in the power of the Mantle of the Expert approach and, in his own way, echoes the importance of faith and belief in a pedagogical creed which was discussed in Chapter 4. Is there a danger that this insistence on one model of curriculum development omits important aspects of young peoples' learning? In History, in particular, the concept of interpretation is a very contentious issue. Whilst the approaches that Kingstone has adopted may well be highly entertaining, are they highly educational? Why is the 'dramatic reveal' such an important component of this approach to creative learning?

Sustaining the changes

Since its inception there have been seven teachers who have remained at the core of the CS team, whilst several newly qualified teachers have joined it latterly. Those colleagues new to the team have been mentored by Ondrie, who has ensured that they understand the pedagogy behind PBL. In addition to this, Ondrie has offered workshops where teaching methodologies have been showcased, as has advanced skills teacher Jane Hewitt, who has enlisted the help of Dorothy Heathcote. There has been discussion about whether or not CS could continue to function in the absence of key members of staff in the team, and the expectation is that it can and will be sustained indefinitely.

CS is now an accepted part of the Year 7 timetable at Kingstone, and thus could be said to be fully embedded. The curriculum model has been honed year on year since 2005, meaning that the way we currently deliver the programme is markedly different to the approach that we took during the pilot. A number of changes have occurred during that time which mean that CS teachers are confident that their work facilitates deeper learning than it did prior to the introduction of the new model.

Establishing a team of practitioners who share Matthew's vision has been crucial to the proliferation of CS. The programme represents such a large proportion of both the teachers' and pupils' timetables that to involve colleagues who are unable or unwilling to approach PBL properly is obviously detrimental. Identifying staff who genuinely wanted to remain part of the CS team and timetabling one teacher to work with a class for its entire 15 hours per fortnight represented a huge step forward for the programme.

The members of staff involved in our thematic curriculum also appear to have undergone a shift in mind-set that has made teaching and learning in CS more effective now than when it was first introduced. Formerly, members of staff viewed the component subjects of CS discretely within units of work, meaning that they explored the geographical elements of a topic in one lesson and the religious or historical links in others. Latterly, however, they have come to regard CS as an entity in its own right. As a result, they feel free to examine the themes in which students display most interest in detail, and those that do not generate enthusiasm in less detail.

Another milestone in the evolution of CS has been recognition of the need for variety in our teaching methods. In CS's infancy there arose a tendency to make use of dramatic

FIGURE 5.11 'Children are much better socially; much better at solving problems; much more willing to take learning on for themselves.'

conventions at times when more traditional methods of learning would have been more effective. Concerns were raised that this was having a detrimental effect on our students' ability to write in a cohesive way, and that too much subject content was being over-looked. Though it is still very difficult to ensure absolute consistency in the spread of learning styles used by the teachers of CS, we believe that we are now providing our pupils with the range of learning opportunities which they need to allow every one of them to flourish.

As Matthew says: 'In a nutshell, the impact of it is very much enhanced relationships in and around the school; the children are much better socially; much better at solving problems; much more willing to take learning on for themselves.'

Questions for consideration

The changes instituted at Kingstone are impressive, with the level of 'buy-in' that staff have shown and the visible leadership of Matthew Milburn. What, though, are the threats to the sustainability of this approach? Given that it requires the constant adaption and responsiveness of teaching staff to potentially new circumstances and contexts every time they teach Cultural Studies, how would you ensure that those staff are constantly fresh and inspired by the challenge they face?

Some futures . . .

CS is by no means a finished article. Though we no longer feel that National Curriculum levelling alone fits the purpose of assessing progress in CS, we are still working to supplement it with a fully cohesive programme of formative and summative assessment.

Following the departure of the first full cohort of students to participate in CS, there have been calls for a full evaluation of the project to determine whether its long-term impact has been a positive one. Completing an objective evaluation will not be easy, as there are those members of staff who believe whole-heartedly in its value and those who remain opposed to it. The aforementioned year group is qualitatively and quantitatively different to those that came before and after it, and the standard of CS delivered during the pilot in 2005, its full introduction in 2006 and subsequent years has varied widely.

There are a number of teachers who would ultimately like to see the principles of CS applied to all of the teaching and learning that takes place at Kingstone. These teachers still seem to be in the minority, however, and they will need to forge links with colleagues outside of this nucleus in order to force the thematic curriculum agenda. It will, hopefully, be the case that if interested parties collaborate and demonstrate success and then disseminate on their knowledge, the take-up of thematic learning will gather momentum.

As Matthew suggests, the crucial influence in its ongoing success will be not only the teacher, but how that teacher views their subject, their pupils and what can be crafted from fusing all the elements in a pedagogy of creativity:

The teacher working with the National Strategies is a joiner and the teacher working with this [Mantle of the Expert] way of working is a proper sculptor. And if you're working with wood you do have to pay attention to where the knots are and you cannot just plane them out because you'll end up breaking your tools and end up with something that looks like a complete dog's breakfast. If you work with those knots, then actually a sculptor will make that into a feature of what it is they are creating and it will be something very beautiful and they will find a way of enabling the wood to live and to take a form which is beautiful in itself. What a joiner will do is cut straight through it.

Moving on and scaling up: how to maintain the momentum?

Matthew has pointed to the ongoing development of the approach, brings its own set of difficulties: how to involve new staff, how to keep the work fresh, how to maintain its quality and also how to extend its reach. This is an unenviable list, particularly bearing in mind the other initiatives the school is expected to engage with: the Personal Learning and Thinking Skills (PLTS) and Building Schools for the Future programme, to name but two national programmes that were, at the time of writing, beginning to impact on the school community. How does your school go about nurturing its important practices when faced with the thrill and enticement – and distraction – of new initiatives?

FIGURE 5.12 Sustaining the transformation in times of multiple national initiatives

Notes

1 http://www.mantleoftheexpert.com/about-moeMantle of the Expert/introduction/what-is-moeMantle of the Expert/.
2 http://www.mantleoftheexpert.com/about-moeMantle of the Expert/introduction/how-does-moeMantle of the Expert-work/.
3 Source: http://college.cengage.com/education/pbl/background.html.
4 http://future.ncsl.org.uk/resources/61_coconstructing_learning.pdf.
5 A sister volume to this book addresses student voice in more detail.

References

Blumenfeld, P., Soloway, E., Marx, R., Krajcik, J., Guzdial, M. and Palincsar, A. (1991) 'Motivating Project-based Learning: Sustaining the Doing, Supporting the Learning', *Educational Psychologist*, 26 (3–4): 369–98.

Bransford, J.D. and Stein, B.S. (1993) *The Ideal Problem Solver*, 2nd edn, New York: Freeman.

Craft, A., Cremin, T., Burnard, P. and Chappell, K. (2007) 'Teacher Stance in Creative Learning: A Study of Progression', *Thinking Skills and Creativity*, 2(2): 136–47.

Vigilant, Resilient and Transformative Change from 0 to 60 in Less than the Time Needed To Bat an Organisational Eye

Thornleigh Salesian College, Bolton

Mick Johnson and Alison Burrowes

Editor's introduction

This chapter demonstrates how staff at Thornleigh Salesian School, a Catholic high school in Bolton, developed programmes which were based on the concept of multiple learning styles to encourage their children's independent learning and thinking skills. The school also engaged with the Personalised Learning Agenda through programmes which focused on developing students' 'learning to learn' skills, providing a new Year 7 curriculum which was characterised by deep learning, cross-curriculum activities and flexibility in timetabling, the use of new technologies and significant school redesign and organisation. It has embraced the personalised learning and thinking skills (PLTS) agenda too, but in a manner which has enabled it to take ownership of that initiative.

Thornleigh Salesian wanted to embrace the opportunity to transform the learning of its students to prepare them for what they saw as an uncertain twenty-first century: and this proved to be a spur to developing a curriculum which placed it pupils at the centre of the creative learning process. Its starting question for the process was: 'What do we want our learners to be like?'

The school context, by Mick Johnson

Thornleigh Salesian College is a large, mixed comprehensive school for the Catholic community of Bolton. It is one of three Catholic schools in the town and the only one with a sixth form. It has a slightly above-average intake for most years in terms of ability and attainment, and in recent years has been producing average or slightly under-average national attainment for most pupils. So our CVA (Contextual Value Added score) has not been what we've wanted for our school.

Twenty-two years ago Thornleigh Salesian changed from a boys' grammar school to a mixed comprehensive school. It has been conservative in character, but during the last seven years alone there has been a significant turnover of leadership in the school and this has had an impact on a number of areas of school improvement. In January 2008, Alison Burrowes took over as head teacher and she quickly assessed the position with colleagues and established a thorough and robust school improvement plan. A person with a strategic and analytical eye, she was not afraid of changing things.

I had joined the school five years previously as Assistant Head Teacher, with a brief for raising achievement in Key Stage 3. That changed with the appointment of Alison, who changed my role to Assistant Head Teacher, Learning and Teaching, with responsibility for developing the curriculum at Key Stage 3.

In terms of the current Key Stage 4 and the Key Stage 5, there has been a great deal of intervention. There has been some clever work with timetables and with groupings; and early entries into exams – for example, in last few years Year 10 all sat English Language GCSE at the end of Year 10 and then dedicated Year 11 to English Literature, whereas previously they had studied the two alongside each other. So there have been interventions of many different kinds. We've also engaged more local authority support than we had done in the past. Whilst some of the short-term and medium-term things that we've done apply particularly to the current exam group, we're mindful that what will really change life chances for the children, and change results, is good teaching in the classroom every day and all the time and in all the subjects.

I was presented with some important decisions: either to focus on results and drive up standards or to adopt a more creative, innovative and risk-taking path. I decided to combine both approaches, addressing both the short-term, immediate needs, but also convinced that the results would improve, with the students developing as independent learners *en route*.

Questions for discussion

Mick presents several factors which contributed to a climate in which curriculum change was being made possible: intervention in the timetable; changes of group sizes and early entry to public exams for example. What factors are present in your school which could contribute to the necessary climate for curriculum change?

The Salesian School Network

Thornleigh Salesian is a Catholic school, linked not only to the Diocese but also to the Salesian's of Don Bosco: an order of priests who follow the work of an Italian cleric in the late nineteenth century who was working in Turin with deprived children in that city. It is the first Catholic school that Mick has worked in. He suggests the school offers a significant difference from other secondary schools with its emphasis on developing the whole child and suggests that this comes about due to it links with the work of Don Bosco and his ideas of what a school should be: an experience of home, playground, school and church.

Cast of characters/actors

Alison Burrowes	Head teacher
Vicky Carberry	Advanced skills teacher
Mick Johnson	Assistant head teacher

Timeline

January 2008	Alison Burrowes appointed as head teacher
September 2008	Management commitment to radically rethink provision. Vicky and I led a team of staff who were to deliver across the whole school
September 2009	Delivery of curriculum implemented

The initial spark: a pot of money at the end of an application rainbow

Our initial involvement with Creative Partnerships (CP) was a tentative one. Our initial interest in applying for a pot of funding led to participation in some one-off and longer-term projects looking to harness and increase the creativity of their staff and students. But this initial interest in funding did not provide us with a rationale for ongoing commitment to developing creative curricula. The major involvement with CP was the development of our creative curriculum for Year 7. We received creative and financial support from CP as well as a 'fresh set of eyes from someone outside of school', which I found reassuring. Reassurance might not sound that valuable a commodity, but when we were thinking of taking a risk and changing things quite a lot, the reassurance that we were involved with a group of people who were experienced in making changes in other schools and who were going to hold our hands through the process was very important.

This led to a consultation process with staff which asked the questions shown in Figure 6.1.

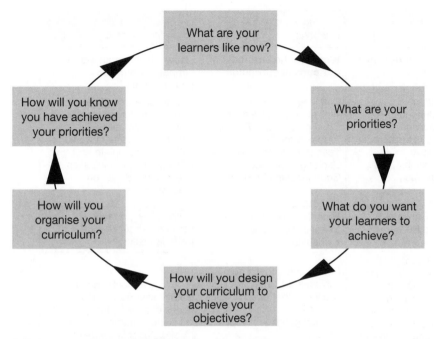

FIGURE 6.1 The questions asked at the start of the innovation process

Questions for discussion

Would these be your questions if you were designing a model for curriculum change? If not, what would you leave out? What would you include?

The struggles in preparing for innovation

One obvious struggle we set ourselves was dealing with the 12-month lead-in period. As well as planning the curriculum and timetable, we also had to carry out a range of consultation processes which had to be carried out with the usual range of stakeholders: staff, parents and the local education authority.

Alison allocated resources which meant that Vicky and I could go off site on eight Friday afternoons, as well as paying for two full days at a local hotel during the course of the year which all staff could attend. This allowed us to develop a shared vision about what all the staff wanted to achieve by the change process, summarised in Figure 6.2.

In early discussions about how we could promote a competency based curriculum we thought about strapping together two or three subjects and following a cross-curricular approach. Usually, this is achieved by knitting together common work between the humanities and English, but I was convinced that we could have more

What are we trying to achieve?	How do we organise learning?	How well are we achieving our aims?
What are our learners like now?	**What are the strengths of our current curriculum?**	**How will we evaluate the impact of our new curriculum?**
Not independent Spoon fed Dependant Weak self managers Lacking in skills Indifferent Lacking initiative Poor organisation Unable to take/use feedback	Challenges Engages Well structured Relevant Good progression Practical Prepares for GCSE Teachers provide flexibility Use of group work Good teaching Traditional	Pupil voice Use of data Retention Commitment Improved behaviour Improved quality of work More HW completed Observation Participation Less dependence on teachers
What do we want our learners to be like?	What features do we need to have in our new curriculum?	What do we need to do to bring about change to our curriculum?
More independent Bring basic skills with them Expressive Confident Risk takers Motivated Developing sophistication Show initiative Reflective Problem solving Organised Engaged Self-evaluative Rounded well balanced citizens	Common approach from subject staff Time Draw together threads across KS Engaging, mixed and diverse Variety Personal investigation and experimentation Cross curricular working	Provide students with basic skills lower down CPD Look at assessment practice Links to primaries – visits Make students aware of learning styles ICT Cross curricular links Risks Progressive framework

FIGURE 6.2 A shared vision of the staff of Thornleigh Salesian

impact if our new curriculum were to stand alone. I recognised, though, that any new curriculum had to be taken out of existing curriculum time, and that there were likely to be winners and losers in this process.

Starting-points

Note the two distinct approaches that Kingstone and Thornleigh Salesian offer in their response to developing a new curriculum. Kingstone knitted together a programme of work between the humanities and English; Thornleigh Salesian wanted a stand-alone approach. What would more likely be successful in your school? The starting-point for the school was the question: 'What are needs of the learners? What do we want our learners to look like in the future?' What starting questions would you use in your school to begin a process of curriculum innovation? Have you asked these questions about your pupils?

The importance of advocating for incremental improvement

Bearing in mind that there are also a lot of things we are doing to increase attainment, we're always looking to where you can get those next few percentage points from, both in terms of the school and for the life chances of the students.

The approach that we wanted to take with the young people was to concentrate on how they learned: we wanted to enable them to understand their learning to a higher degree and to develop their metacognition skills. We consequently had to justify why we were taking 20 per cent out of the Year 7 year timetable to pursue this, and we had to convince staff that in four years' time, when these young people would be in Year 11, our results will have gone up.

Questions for discussion

Learning 'to a higher degree' and developing 'metacognition skills' might sound like attractive goals to aim for. But what would they mean in your school? How would you define learning 'to a higher degree'? What might that kind of learning look like? And what kind of teaching strategies would you need to put in place to bring about those metacognition skills?

Alison knew that she had to ensure that parents understood what the school was aiming to do and why. She led various presentations which communicated plans to parents and was also able to demonstrate how they had created some flexible learning spaces in the school which would be needed for the curriculum to be delivered: knocking walls down, buying portable and flexible ICT equipment, for example. A particular challenge was persuading the governors to agree to the investment in a substantial amount of resources when no one was able to provide them any assurance as to what the outcomes were going to be.

Conditions which encouraged the changes to take hold

Other changes in the school were influencing how likely this new Year 7 curriculum was to take root and grow. The decision had been taken to move from a 25-period week to a 30-period week. This had grown out of the need to increase personalisation at Key Stage 4. However, it presented a series of challenges: we are a sports specialist college, so reducing our PE curriculum time was not an option; and as the school is also a faith school, neither was reducing our RE curriculum time. And we certainly weren't going to reduce time for our maths, English and other core subjects.

So we looked at the school's day and chopped a bit off the lunch break; we removed a form period; we changed the times of the day and we went from 25 periods a week to 30 periods.

But we knew too that even if there were going to be more occasions in the week when the children had lessons, some people were going to gain from this process and

FIGURE 6.3 Something needs to change – asking the students

some people were going to lose, in terms minutes of curriculum time over a week. But for a lot of subjects, particularly the core subjects, we were able to give more lessons in the week. This gave us room in Year 7, when we went from 25 to 30 periods, so that 5 periods immediately became available to teach the new curriculum.

I needed six periods to do what we wanted to do, so we subsumed ICT completely within the new curriculum so there were no stand-alone ICT or citizenship lessons. History and geography each lost a lesson, but every other subject maintained the number of lessons they had had, or even increased them. These changes are being monitored, however: curriculum innovation here isn't a one-way process to a promised land, but more a process of planning, testing, revising and revisiting the vision, with a view to seeing how it can best be delivered.

Questions for discussion

Mick describes a thorough, almost surgical, approach to changing structures and processes in the school in order to generate the timetable space for the new curriculum to emerge. But what is your assessment of the apparent privileging of certain subjects over others? In this context, some sets of knowledge seem to be more important than others. Is that the case in your school too? If you were to attempt a similar kind of process, what subjects would be sacrosanct and which could be sacrificed in the quest for a new curriculum? And why?

Consequently, the resistance to the changes we were proposing was limited. We could assure colleagues who were anxious about the proposals that the changes would have minimal effects on their timetable. Ironically, the sites of most anticipated resistance (ICT and citizenship – given their disappearance as discrete entities within the Year 7 timetable) ended up being particularly enthusiastic to participate in the scheme. Heads of both ICT and citizenship agreed that the teaching of their subjects should be seamless and should be cross curricular across the school: so this new Year 7 curriculum supported their pedagogical principles too, albeit at the expense of discrete teaching times in the timetable.

Pace of change: what's realistic for you?

Mick refers to the work of John Kotter (1990) as being an important resource in their approach to change management. His work is built upon promoting eight steps of change management:

Step One: Create urgency.
Step Two: Form a powerful coalition.
Step Three: Create a vision for change. When you first start thinking about change, there will probably be many great ideas.
Step Four: Communicate the vision.
Step Five: Remove obstacles.
Step Six: Create short-term win.
Step Seven: Build on the change.
Step Eight: Anchor the changes in corporate culture.

Can you identify in this story how Kotter's work has been used to affect curriculum change at the school? One school's manageable change is another school's innovatory change, and for some schools which may have spent considerably longer working within a culture of innovation and change – those which were prepared to burn the QCA guidelines for example – the changes being proposed by Mick and his colleagues at Thornleigh Salesian may look modest by comparison. But if you were to restructure the timetable in your school, what subjects would you be able to lose? Or incorporate into other areas? Are there ways in which you could release another hour in the day for learning? Are these kinds of calculations the best or most important way of talking about curriculum development?

The Four Learning Habits: interpreting nationally driven initiatives

Whilst there was a period of careful planning of a new Year 7 curriculum over eight to ten months of the academic year in 2008/09, at the start of the academic year 2009/10 we also introduced a step change in the Year 7 curriculum: introducing the Four Learning Habits (Figure 6.4).

The concept of the Four Learning Habits is a language of curriculum development in the school which, whilst recognising national moves to promote personalised learning and thinking skills (PLTS), has also enabled us to take ownership of that initiative.

FIGURE 6.4 The four learning habits

Questions for discussion

How would you evaluate these learning habits? What are their strengths and weaknesses? How do they fit within the Hargreaves gateways of personalised learning of:

- Assessment for learning;
- Learning to learn;
- Student voice;
- Curriculum characterised by deep learning, cross-curriculum activities and flexibility in timetabling;
- New technologies;
- School design and organisation, with school leaders seen as organisational redesigners;
- Advice and guidance;
- Mentoring and coaching;
- Workforce development, and in particular the use of adults other than teachers to complement the work of teachers?

PLTS are not a curriculum as such but a set of outcomes which you will produce if you've got your curriculum right.

I think we have taken a courageous move not to explicitly use the language of PLTS but to use the language of our Four Learning Habits, whilst being clear about what we want our children to become: independent enquirers, effective participators in team work and reflective learners who can understand how they learn best.

This entailed focusing on how children learn as well as what they learn. So, as well as promoting transferable skills we also wanted to increase opportunities for children to collaborate, particularly through the use of Kagan Structures, which we used as a vehicle to develop more sophisticated group and collaborative working.

Kagan Structures develop group work and collaborative work. They're based around getting the young people used to collaborating with each other in pairs and in larger groups and giving teachers easy ways to do this. It isn't about doing a whole lesson of group work, but lots of quick little things, like getting people to turn to their neighbours and discuss certain things in a certain way and giving them structures to do this, so that the pupils understand what they are doing and how it helps their learning.

We suggested that staff should use more collaboration and group work to encourage more independent working by the pupils. But we also realised that the pupils needed a certain amount of training: they needed to have good group work modelled to them and explained to them. That's not too hard a job because they are coming out of primary school, where they do it a lot anyway, but we did feel that, through this curriculum, we could try tp make sure that by the end of Year 7 the young people were better able to work in groups.

What are Kagan Structures?[1]

Kagan Structures are step-by-step instructional strategies designed by Spencer Kagan and promoted by the private company Kagan Publishing and Professional Development. They are intended to develop processes of cooperative learning and increase student engagement and cooperation.

Questions for discussion

Whilst Kagan Structures seem to fit within a personalised learning agenda, they are also the result of many years of refinement of a particular product and are sold on the marketplace as such. They are about personalisation, but also are a market commodity which can be 'bought off the shelf'. But does this matter? How important is it for a school to design its own route and its own curriculum if it wants to place its students at the heart of creative learning?

FIGURE 6.5 Collaboration and group work encourages independent learning

From habits to practice

We developed the Four Learning Habits through a structure of six non-sequential modules which are entitled: Olympic Experience; Thornleigh's Kitchen; Eco Village; Rhythm and Racket; Learning through Adventure and Our Town (Figure 6.6).

We have two groups working in parallel on any one of the modules and two colleagues delivering it, and they rotate around these six modules. They are not hierarchical and children don't need to have done one before the other, but there is a spiral curriculum within the module based around our interpretation of PLTS which we distilled into what we call learning habits:

- self-awareness;
- planning and handling information;
- team working;
- working with others.

Whatever the children do in the modules is based around developing those skills. The content of the modules has made them engaging and interesting and as true to life as we can make them – important, we believe, when it comes to motivating children to learn.

Planning	Handling information
I am able to	I am able to
• Set goals and personal targets • See what problems there may be • Decide what needs to be done in what order • Think of different ways to solve a problem • Use a wide range of resources • Organise myself and others • Keep a check on how I and the group are doing • Change and improve my ideas as I work	• Use key points to reach a conclusion • Summarise situations and progress • Ask questions to find out more • Identify different points of view • Pick out details and identify the purpose of the information • Use information to persuade others
Working with others	**Self-awareness**
I am able to	I am able to
• Listen and show other people's points of view • Reach agreements maturely • Take part in group discussions and make my point heard • Work well with others and take different roles in the group • Work well on my own but ask for help when I need it • Take other people's feelings into account • Communicate with different types of people	• Accept praise and constructive criticism • Learn from my mistakes and keep on trying • Take time to reflect when I am frustrated • Take risks • Understand how I learn and how I can use this to grow • Stay focused and concentrate • Create my ideal learning conditions • Learn from others and the way they learn • Make links between things I have learnt and done

FIGURE 6.6 The modular structure to develop the four learning habits

Questions for discussion

The model proposed here of six separate modules is deceptively easy to the eye. But how problems can you foresee with its delivery and what kind of student experience do you think would be typical? How could you assess pupils' progression through these modules? Does it matter that there is no apparent narrative thread or explicit logical cohesion between them?

Pupils follow the modules in five-week cycles. Each module has sub-goals leading towards a final product or presentation or performance. Pupils rotate through the modules and staff stay with each module. We did consider one member of staff delivering all the modules throughout the year, which would have had benefits in terms of transition: for one day a week children would have experienced a real primary model where they were staying with one person. It would also have had spin-offs for colleagues in terms of their own creativity and adaptability in having to teach outside their own specialism. In the end, though, we allocated individual staff to specific modules so that they could become expert in that module.

Learning to learn days: introducing students to the programme

The beginning of the modular sequence is prefaced with core 'learning to learn' days in which everybody follows some units on mind mapping and on multiple intelligences.

This means that children are armed with some basic metacognition background. After this they begin participating in the carrousel of modules as follows.

Questions for discussion

The beginning of this process is based on the validity of theories such as multiple intelligences. Given the difficulties and unreliabilities of these theories (discussed in the Introduction), what are the risks of relying on such theories in developing a model such as this one? Is it important that children are aware that they have some background knowledge of metacognition?

The Olympic Experience

The Olympic Experience asks the young people to take on the role of a country bidding to host a future Olympic games. They look at what the Olympic games are and the Olympic ideal and the role of sport. This picks up on our own specialism as a sports college, opens up an aspect of global citizenship and helps children to find out about these different countries. They look at settlement issues; they look at how to create an Olympic village; how to plan things out; they look at news and media issues; and at one point they switch from being a team bidding for the Olympics to being a media team

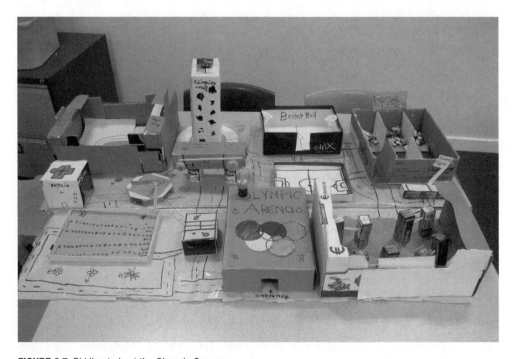

FIGURE 6.7 Bidding to host the Olympic Games

from a country at the Olympics, handling breaking news items such as a failed drugs test or an injury to a star athlete.

Thornleigh's Kitchen

Thornleigh's Kitchen initially started as an enterprise/home technology topic where the children would spend half the module planning and designing a menu. We also intended to provide a restaurant at the end of the module for both staff and pupils. So it would look at cooking as well as the human resources involved in running a restaurant and the design of menu, layout and so on. We visited several local restaurants to talk to them about how to run a business, but this eventually evolved into providing a Christmas market, the end product of which would be the creation and marketing of luxury foodhampers. The skills of the colleagues involved have, meant there has always been a food aspect to the project but the focus on business and enterprise has been fore-grounded during the project's evolution.

The Eco Village

The Eco Village module is about planning a sustainable settlement, looking at the issues of sustainability and investigating them and how they can communicate messages on sustainability and environmental awareness. This module lost a science teacher at the beginning of the process, which proved to be quite crucial. The science teacher was meant to work alongside a music teacher and lead the module, but I lost her at half term because of long-term absence and another colleague has had to pick that up. This has been a difficult process.

Rhythm and Racket

Rhythm and Racket is the module that has had the most demonstrable impact. It looks at performance. Children look at all aspects of performance, such as sound, lighting and set design. Central to the module were the creation of a piece of music and a piece of movement around the theme of man and machine. We take pupils to the Museum of Science and Industry in Manchester, where the museum staff get the engine room running so that the pupils can see and hear it all. This work is interpreted by a drummer, who develops drumming workshops with the children around the sounds of the engine room.

Learning through Adventure

Learning through Adventure is very heavily angled towards personal development – self-awareness and the team-working aspects of our learning habits. The school is fortunate in that it has a site which has plenty of grass in and around it. Pupils aim to complete two building tasks around the school site.

Our Town

Our Town looks at Bolton and finds out what pupils know about their town, and the pupils then make presentations on the topic. On one occasion they linked this work to Bolton's bid for city status, so they had to come up with a persuasive presentation to convince people that Bolton deserved to be a city.

For me, one of the interesting things about this module is that it's shown me how poor children's research skills can be. I appreciate that Google can be a fantastic tool, but it's also a crippling one because it doesn't enable the children ask the right questions. This has meant that some of the pupils have not progressed in their understanding about Bolton. They've not gained knowledge; they've simply fallen back upon the knowledge of Bolton that they already had. So we have needed to develop their research skills, their web intelligence and their internet searching so they can be more effective as independent enquirers.

This research issue highlights one of the biggest headaches teachers have had in delivering the programme: mapping the progression of the children in developing their skills. When the children go from one module to another their teachers have to know quite quickly about how children's skills have developed, so that they do not start at too low a level. Given that the skills in question can sometimes be quite intangible, this is not an easy task. It has proved to be a conundrum for some teachers. The question of how much progress is being made is something which we are still wrestling with.

FIGURE 6.8 Students' presentations of their home town, Bolton

Tracking traditional notions of progress through non-traditional curricula

It has been difficult to track pupils through this modular structure: finding useful evidence of change is not so straightforward a process, given that the school is accustomed to traditional forms of teaching. One of the problems is that colleagues outside of the creative curriculum don't know enough about what the children are doing. A teacher of a history or geography Year 7 group could traditionally see how a group of children were progressing across the year in parallel to what was happening in the creative curriculum: but at the start of the programme, they didn't have that view.

Whilst the teachers in the new curriculum see all the children in their own five-week modules and can determine progression over that time, it is difficult to gain an overview during the whole programme of how a pupil has progressed. This has been a risky process for the school and, given the complexities of tracking and measuring progression, there is a bigger risk that the whole venture could implode under the weight of the expectation and scrutiny that bears down on it. There is a lot at stake, not just for teachers, but for the Year 7 children who are participating in this new, untried venture.

We address these challenges and keep staff, pupils and parents on track through regular self-review, peer review and teacher assessment throughout the planning and delivery phases of the curriculum. I also constantly find ways to remind staff of the need to make the changes, and the length of time that will be required. This has entailed facilitating discussions with staff through INSET sessions about how they saw pupils at the start of the process, what they wanted them to be like and what the staff themselves wanted to change – as well as introducing staff new to the school to the mission they had embarked upon. However, despite these difficulties, colleagues have told me anecdotally that children are better at group work; that they are calmer; and that they are more civilised, for want of a better word, in class.

But despite the tensions and conflicts, the changes brought about by the new curriculum and the promotion of the Learning Habits model have been sufficiently positive for the head teacher and the school leadership to decide that they should now pursue the language of Learning Habits throughout the school.

Questions for discussion

Research, simulation and 'real world' learning opportunities are some of the key themes of the Four Habits of Learning approach. Are there any other key themes which are common to the modules in this approach? Would you say that there are essential themes which all students should have to engage with in this approach? How would you go about assessing achievement in this type of model? How would you develop this approach in your own school context? What counts as learning in this model?

What next?

Whilst the short-term needs of the change process were addressed through various retunings of the schools management systems – amending timetables, regroupings and arranging for early entries into exams – these are procedures which are common to many schools which are looking to improve their performance in public examinations over a short period of time.

But we have also been mindful that what will really change life chances for the children – and change results – is good teaching in the classroom every day, all the time, in all the subjects, throughout the whole school.

This has led to a commitment to developing longer-term, more embedded change which is built on approaches which develop creative learning and teaching alongside improving standards and attainment.

Matters for consideration: what do you want your learners to look like?

Mick pointed to the need to involve a team of credible champions or a specialist team in the design of the curriculum who then spread the initiative across all curriculum areas and across their departments. Can you identify potential champions/specialists in your school who could begin this process with you?

Note

1 http://www.kaganonline.com/free_articles/dr_spencer_kagan/ASK38.php.

Reference

Kotter, J. (1990) *A Force for Change: How Leadership Differs from Management*, New York: Free Press.

Professional Development Sessions for Groups

Let's Imagine . . .

Nick Owen and Ethel Sanders

This chapter aims to offer ideas, approaches and, above all, questions about how you would go about that process of placing your students at the heart of creative learning.

It is drawn from the discussion questions in the chapters of this book. It is clear from the case studies that this type of change of focus does not happen overnight; that it cannot be sustained through the valiant efforts of one individual alone; and that the road ahead is not without its struggles and setbacks. However, it is also clear that because there is a lot at stake and the rewards are potentially huge – for pupils, for teachers and for the wider community – engaging with the process and committing to it in the long term are perhaps the only guarantees that these rewards will be forthcoming.

This chapter is offered as a model for a series of continuing professional development sessions to be held with a staff group – either within one school or across a cluster of schools. It is essential of course that representatives from the school's senior management are involved in this process – but it is important, as we have seen, that ownership is spread from the head (and the heart) of the school, throughout its whole body of pupils, staff, governors and wider stakeholders. So the more stakeholders you can get involved in this process, the better.

It is structured around four headings:

1. How your school ethos and culture can contribute to placing students at the heart of creative learning.

2. What your school wants your learners to look like.

3. How children's communities and local funds of knowledge can support the development of personalised learning.

4. The roles and practices of teachers in placing students at the heart of creative learning in a standards-driven educational environment.

These headings are intended to offer insights and questions which should lead to a series of action points – or pledges – which your school will sign up to and commit to throughout the process.

1

Purpose

To consider how your school ethos and culture can contribute to placing students at the heart of creative learning.

Time required

1 hour

Participants

Whole staff

Outline of activity

Work in small groups using the case studies to find out the ways in which other schools have articulated their understanding of their school ethos and culture. Sharing of key points and comparing with current practice in the school.

Resources

- Copies of the six case studies.
- Post-It notes in three colours.
- Large sheets of plain paper.
- A whiteboard marked out in three columns labelled Culture, Ethos, Risk action for course leader to display Post-It notes.

Instructions

- Form six groups. Each group has a copy of one of the case studies and Post-It notes in three colours.
- Each group reads one of the case studies to find out how school ethos and culture have impacted on its desire to place students at the centre of the creative learning process. Feed back to each other within the group, with leader recording on Post-It notes, using a different colour (agree this across all the groups) for each of the following three aspects:
  - the status given to children's own backgrounds and the wider community;

- the pressures to produce a creative curriculum or raise standards;
- tendencies to risk-averseness or risk-tolerance;

■ Groups place the Post-It notes in the relevant column on whiteboard. Course leader reviews findings.

■ Each group discusses how 'centred' pupils are in the learning at its school and thinks of one way to re-centre pupils, and the motivation for their idea. Feedback to group leader, who leads discussion on the pros and cons of each idea. If possible, reach a consensus on one pledge to be implemented.

Further development

Using the findings from the case studies as a prompt, the leadership team could produce an action plan for implementing the agreed-upon idea for the re-centring of pupils at the heart of creative learning in the school.

2

Purpose

To identify what your school wants its learners to look like.

Time required

1½ hours

Participants

Middle/senior leaders

Outline of activity

Consideration of the motives for developing personalised learning and how school leaders translate motivation into action.

Resources

■ Download of Sir Ken Robinson's talk, 'Do Schools Kill Creativity?' http://www.ted.com/talks/lang/eng/ken_robinson_says_schools_kill_creativity.html.

■ Copies of the six case studies so that each group of six has a copy of each one.

■ Large sheets of blank paper and Post-It notes. Pens. Blu-Tack.

Instructions

- 20 minutes – Watch the film of Ken Robinson's talk, 'Do Schools Kill Creativity?'
- 20 minutes – Groups discuss the basic premise of the talk, whether or not they agree with it, giving reasons for their view. Group spokesperson presents summary of views.
- 30 minutes – Each person in the group reads one of the six case studies. Identify the school's vision for what it wants its learners to look like. Write the vision on a Post-It note and place all the notes on a large sheet of blank paper. Course leader to read out visions. How well do they resonate with the views of Ken Robinson?
- 30 minutes – Each person in the group finds three key leadership actions in their case study that enabled personalised learning to be developed. Share these within the group. Group spokesperson to feedback to course leader. What actions are common to all the case study schools?

3

Purpose

To consider the ways in which children's communities and local funds of knowledge can support the development of personalised learning.

Time required

1 hour

Participants

Whole staff

Outline of activity

Use the case studies to:

- dentify the various forms of engagement with the local community that are employed to support the development of personalised learning and the conditions necessary for successful collaboration;
- consider how use of local funds of knowledge could be enhanced or extended within participants' school;
- identify where new and different sources of knowledge and capital might be in your school's locality.

Resources

- Copies of the six case studies to enable each of six groups to study one of them.
- Paper and pens for each group.
- A whiteboard marked out with a 6 x 6 grid – 1 column for each school and 1 row for each form of collaboration as detailed in the instructions.

Instructions

- Form six groups (one group per case study), with each person being given a copy of the assigned case study.
- Groups read their case study to find the various ways in which the school has used local community funds of knowledge to develop creative practice. Feed back to group leader, who will record examples of collaborative practice:
  - with other schools;
  - with community organisations;
  - with external agents, e.g. artists; and
  - the conditions necessary for successful collaboration.
- Feed back to group leader, who will record findings from each school on a grid marked out on a whiteboard.
- Groups discuss collaborative practice within their school using findings as prompts. Think of a way in which collaboration could be enhanced.
- Feed back to group leader, who will review suggestions.

Further development

Leadership group to take an agreed suggestion for greater collaborative practice and produce an action plan for implementation, using the case studies as a resource if necessary.

4

Purpose

To consider the roles and practices of teachers in placing students at the heart of creative learning in a standards-driven educational environment.

Time required

2½ hours

Participants

Head teachers, deputy head teachers and senior leaders.

Outline of activity

- To discuss the challenge of personalised learning within a context of centrally mandated accountability and a results-based agenda.
- To examine how teachers' practice will change in a personalised learning environment.

Resources

- Download film of *Systems Upgrade* from Creative Partnerships.
- Copies of the book Introduction – one per person.
- Large sheets of plain paper and marker pens for course leader. Pens and paper for participants.

Instructions

- 20 minutes – Watch the film of *Systems Upgrade*. Discuss the issues regarding the role of teachers in the era of personalised learning.
- 30 minutes – Arrange participants in six groups of at least two and not more than eight. Each group to read the book Introduction and, with the film in mind, consider how teachers' roles might change when students are placed at the centre of the creative learning process.
- 30 minutes – Each group to study one of the case studies and identify the changes teachers demonstrate in developing personalised learning practice. Group leader to note the key findings.
- 20 minutes – Groups to feed back to course leader, who will record key pedagogical knowledge on a large sheet of paper and review.
- 20 minutes – Groups feed back to course leader, who will record key findings on a large sheet of plain paper. (Course leader arranges to have information from group feedback transcribed onto A4 paper and copied for each participant to take away.)
- Individual participants to think of an action they can take to develop their own capacity in working within a personalised learning environment.

Further development

A personal informal audit of knowledge, skills and attributes, based on information and examples in the book, can be undertaken. An aspect for further development can be identified and a learning journal kept to record progress. (See section on learning journals.)

Individual study – reflective learning journals

Keeping a journal is a very useful aid in individual professional development. The purposes of keeping a journal are as follows:

- To note evidence of practice within the area of chosen study.
- To critically reflect on the practice noted.
- To record ideas for developing practice.
- To note questions you may have.
- To note sources of information related to the subject – documents, literature, research papers, websites etc.
- To critically reflect on the accessed information.
- To reflect on and critically evaluate any change that has been implemented.
- To reflect on and note developments in your learning.

A reflective learning journal is not merely a description of observations but should record the outcomes of your questioning of practice and information rather than accepting it at face value. The process of taking time to reflect and question is important in challenging received assumptions and orthodoxies. Organising your journal is a matter of personal preference but it may help to arrange it in sections based on the afore-mentioned purposes. Record on one page and keep the facing page blank to add comments, questions, etc. as they arise. Try to set aside time each day for reflection, noting critical points. The journal can be regarded as a way of 'brainstorming' with yourself. It can be useful to record thoughts gleaned through the bouncing around of ideas between you and a colleague. A small dictaphone might be a useful aid to recording your thoughts immediately during the day when you are 'on the go' so that they can be written up later when you have time to reflect on them. From time to time review the whole of your journal and note changes to thinking as well as learning that has occurred.

A useful guide to keeping a learning journal is:

Moon, J. (1999) *Learning Journals: A Handbook for Academics, Students and Professional Development*, London: Kogan Page.

Index